ISBN 0 7158 0800 1

First edition 1982

Published by EP Publishing Limited, East Ardsley, Wakefield,
West Yorkshire, WF3 2JN.

Design: Krystyna Hewitt
Illustrations: Douglas Hewitt

Photographic credits
All-Sport/Tony Duffy: page 29
Austrian National Tourist Office/Foto Sündhofer: page 104 (right)
Findlay Davidson: page 9
Elan: page 65
Linda Lemieux: inside back cover
Stan Palmer: pages 11, 55 (right)

All other photographs by John Shedden

Text set in 10/11pt Cheltenham Book by Waveney Typesetters, Norwich
and printed and bound in Great Britain by Butler & Tanner Ltd,
Frome and London

Skilful Skiing

Skilful Skiing

John Shedden

Director of Coaching
The English Ski Council

EP Publishing Limited

Acknowledgements

I would like to thank all my colleagues in the English Ski Council for their friendship and enthusiasm, not only in the development of our coaching scheme but also with my research for this book, which began way back in 1970.

My special thanks go to Stan Palmer for his support and his contribution to the chapter on 'Body preparation'. Also to Alan Hughes, Karina Zarod, Alan Hole, Colin Whiteside, Lloyd Bowen, the two Daves, F. and C., and Olive Newson for their faith in me, and to my good friend John Atkinson for his 'coaching'.

For their special help with my photographs, I would like to thank Stig Strand, Bengt Fjaellberg and the Swedish Ski Team and their coach Jean-Pierre Chattelard; Bojan Križaj, Boris Strel of the Jugoslavian Ski Team, and their coach Philip Gardener; Peter Popangelov, Mitko Hadjiev and Georgi Milushev of the Bulgarian Ski Team; and Philippa Eades, Fiona Pulsford, Sarah Lewis and members of the English Ski Squad.

For their help with the production of the photographs, I am very grateful to Thomson Holidays and the Grindelwald Tourist Office, to Olympus (U.K.) Limited for their assistance with a motor drive and 35-mm camera, and to Canon for their assistance with the high-speed Super 8 cine camera which has enabled me to study the movements of skiers.

Contents

Foreword
David Vine

We were sitting around a blazing log fire in the prettiest ski lodge you could imagine. The expensive and latest fashion *après-ski* outfits were everywhere, adorning the beautiful people, bronzed, handsome and glamorous. Outside, just a few flakes of new snow were falling and the forecast was for a perfect day tomorrow. Inside the world was perfect as well, everyone talking about 'that great run I had today high up on the sun-kissed mountain . . .'

Or at least, that's how you might imagine the scene. In fact, it was very different. Very very different. The fire had gone out—about a month ago—and the people weren't all that beautiful. As for the *après-ski* wear, that consisted of sweaters which might not stand another wash, and track suit bottoms that had obviously been 'borrowed'. Outside it was raining, and inside if a skier wasn't nursing a pulled muscle, he would be complaining about his skis and everything else in creation. It had been a terrible day. And where were we?—in the company of the most famous ski racers in the world, the élite of the world cup, the men who today command an audience of millions on television screens in almost every nation, including of course Great Britain where the BBC's *Ski Sunday* has become one of the most watched ski programmes anywhere. So you're now asking what had happened to all that 'newspaper gossip column high life'. What about the famous 'Snow Show' and the often quoted 'White Circus'?.

This was it. The people who make the White Circus roll, the performers, think of only one thing (almost) when they're not racing. And that is: why they didn't race faster last time and how they're going to next time. There's always a reason even though it might be more than just a little difficult to find after hours of discussion with the coaches and trainers. 'Where was that hundredth of a second or so lost? Why did we lose the line on what looked to be the simplest of turns?' They'll go on talking until a possible solution is found and hope that the solution is the right one when it comes to the morning—and the next one, and the next . . . These are the perfectionists which is why they're the stars of what is for me the most exciting sport in the world.

Make no mistake—it's going to be exciting for you if you're one of the thousands who'll be trying it all for the first time this winter. For a moment or two it will probably be terrifying as well! And although skiing is about having fun, if that element of danger wasn't there, the fun wouldn't be half as good when you manage to get it right. When you're on those skis and travelling at . . . well at least travelling forwards, you'll be Franz Klammer, Steve

Podborski and Peter Mueller all rolled into one, in your mind. But whoever you've transformed yourself into, despite a body position which is causing your instructor to tear his hair out, don't for goodness sake try to take the impersonation too far.

None of us who saw it happen will ever forget the most frightening crash in the last few years of the World Cup. It happened at Wengen on the famous Lauberhorn, one of the classics of all ski racing. The Swiss champion, Peter Mueller, had been drawn number one on the day, for some skiers the worst position of any in the top 15, the seeds. Mueller was travelling faster than anyone had ever done in the history of this great event. His time was magnificent and he took the icy 'S' near the bottom in style. But this year the left hander into the steep finish had been widened on the right, in theory to make it safer. Mueller knew he had more room in which to make the turn at over 80 mph. That meant he kept the power on longer. And as he flew into sight of the massive crowd at the bottom and of all the commentators, he was obviously out of control. You could see him fighting, in the air, to throw his body forwards and regain the balance he'd so hopelessly lost. He didn't. And at 80 mph, Peter Mueller crashed through the bales, the fence, and the people who had no chance of moving in the tenth of a second or so it had all taken.

But—and what a big BUT it was, Mueller had done nothing more than damage a shoulder and was racing again before very long. It wasn't just luck because when we examined the incident with the aid of the marvels of modern television, slow motion replay and freeze frame, we saw that Mueller had, in the very last fraction of a second, turned his body into the fence taking the force of the crash on his back and shoulder. Had he not, he would have gone in head first and despite the crash helmet, he could well have given ski racing that season its worst moment.

Call it what you like—expertise, instinct, trained reaction or some other quality, but it was a quality that only the perfectionist can enjoy. It takes years to acquire—and all those hours spent talking in front of the burned out log fire in that none-too glamorous hotel room coupled with the hours and hours on the slopes help to produce it.

On your run down the mountain (of course it will be the Lauberhorn when you tell the story in the evening), enjoy the fun of being a race star. But keep it in your mind and you may keep the skis on your feet! What will certainly help is this book written by my good friend John Shedden, respected all over the winter world as an authority and technical expert. For those already enjoying the fun of the mountains, there's more than enough in what John has written, and the book's so well illustrated, to give you even more pleasure and even more skill. And I wouldn't be at all surprised if in a year or two from now I'm commentating on *Ski Sunday* and saying, 'And here he (and she the next day) comes to the finish . . . and that's the winner'. I hope I get your name right!

Introduction

Almost every year we see the publication of books aimed at introducing newcomers to skiing. Most of them are very good in part, and many of them attempt to teach the beginner how to ski. But reading without practice is of little value, and skiing ability will only be developed by 'having a go'—by skiing. This should be done under the guidance of a good ski instructor.

I say 'guidance' because however good the ski instructor is, he or she cannot do the learning for the pupils, but can only guide them and show them a way forward.

Progress only comes to those who take some responsibility for their own learning. Real and lasting improvement and enjoyment will come to those who have clear and reasonable 'goals' and who are willing to help themselves achieve them, rather than put the responsibility entirely onto the ski instructor to *teach them*.

My aim in writing this book is to offer, to keen skiers who have already learned how to make linked turns, the goal of *skilful skiing*, and to provide guidance towards this goal through insight into the *fundamental constituents* of the skilful performances of advanced recreational and competitive skiers.

Progress will be measured by increased control, efficiency and versatility in recreational skiing, and improved times in races for competitive skiers.

Skilful skiing will increase the exhilaration of descents and enable greater *enjoyment* of the *sensations* involved as the body moves in closer harmony with nature in exciting and often truly awesome settings.

Chapter one

The Goal: Skilful Skiing

Ski schools

The easiest and probably the best way to begin skiing is by joining a ski school. As you progress, however, you should select your school and your instructor carefully, because there can be pitfalls in following the instructor's *dogma* blindly.

The value of the ski school class is that here you will make new friends, you will be spurred on by others' successes and consoled by your colleagues' failures. The ski instructor will do all he can to keep you safe while you are learning to cope with your recently acquired, heavy, long and awkward feet. The knowledge that 'you are not alone' will help you through those moments when you just 'can't get it together' and sharing your excitement and exhilaration of the movement possibilities that skiing provides is often a pleasure in itself.

Another value of ski schools lies in the expertise and knowledge of its staff—its instructors. They will know the mountain like the backs of their hands and the teaching method they use will have been well tried and tested.

The good instructor will be able to use his experience and expertise to help you as an individual person but, unfortunately, the poor ski instructor will not see you as an individual but simply as another customer who has come to learn the 'latest ski technique'—the latest *ski school dogma*.

Whilst skiing is a sport to those of us who participate, it is, in fact, an industry in those centres where people holiday. Indeed, in some countries, Austria for example, it forms a major part of the economy.

A ski class enjoying group 'formation' skiing

In Austria, the product 'Austrian ski technique' is a major part of the economy

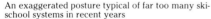

An exaggerated posture typical of far too many ski-school systems in recent years

All the major skiing holiday nations have organised commercial agencies providing ski instruction, using methods which differentiate each nation from another by an emphasis on either selected ski techniques or the sequence in which 'exercises' are taught.

It is in this area of nationalistic ski school dogma that keen skiers can be misled and eventually become disenchanted.

Ski schools are selling a 'product'—the 'so and so way of skiing'. The good ski instructor (salesman) tailors the product to fit the skier (customer) but the poor salesman will insist that the customer buys the product as it is.

I overheard just such an instructor, in an Alpine ski resort, tell a pupil in his class (a group of people who had taken lessons from this same instructor for several years): 'You must not turn like that—we do not teach that way any more.' The ski school had decided to change its methods, adopt a new dogma and the salesman was now trying to sell the 'latest method'.

Fortunately for the class, however, the pupil in question countered this 'sales pitch' by reminding the instructor that he (the pupil) had only ever been taught by this one instructor, and since last year's holiday, he had thought only of perfecting this particular technique. Now he proudly demonstrated his practised ability, only to be told it was 'wrong'.

'In that case,' said the pupil, 'I want my money back! Either for

12

last year or this year, you can't have it both ways.'

This was an enlightened ending to an all-too-familiar process, whereby inexperienced ski instructors (but they all look the same in their ski-school uniforms, don't they?)

- through an inappropriate emphasis on only some aspects of ski technique,
- through an exaggeration of body shapes so that they become awkward and worse-than-useless 'ski positions'
- and through an over-emphasis on the technique aspects of skiing, often out of context with appropriate application of those movements to either the body of the skier or the nature of the terrain,

can *distort the learner's perception* of what skiing really is.

If you are going to take responsibility for your own learning, you must be able to discriminate the good instructor from the not-so-good ones and also understand the *essence* of what he or she is guiding you through.

Ski schools may change their methods and techniques, but, to evaluate these changes, it must be borne in mind that:

neither the mountains,

nor the humans who venture into them,

nor the 'laws' which govern the motion of those humans in the mountains

have changed very much since skiing began.

The nature of the *surfaces* of the mountains—the pistes—have changed, as more and more skiers descend the slopes.

Instructors' and coaches' *understanding* of both the nature of humans and the 'laws' which govern their motion has changed

Some traditional ski schools still teach with methods which were devised when skiers had to climb mountains on foot

too, although, unfortunately, not as quickly or effectively as the real changes which have occurred in *equipment*—boots, skis, sticks and clothing.

New technology has allowed equipment to be developed which enables both greater and different forms of control to be exerted over that equipment by modern skiers.

This accounts for the major, useful changes in techniques and methods which have emerged.

The other major influence on 'method' has been the changing reasons why people ski and what they want to achieve with their technical ability.

Some traditional ski schools still teach with methods which were devised when skiers had to climb mountains on foot and then descend slowly and carefully in deep snow, with boots and bindings which gave little support. Other—ultra modern—ski schools accept the use of lifts, the support which modern equipment gives, and teach with methods designed to enable their pupils to negotiate short, shallow pistes, skiing parallel, as soon as possible.

Both methods are based on an assumption that the pupil wants to use his skiing in the mountains in a very particular manner, and under the circumstances surrounding that method. This may not always be so.

As a keen skier, you will have your own reasons for wanting to ski, and these reasons will change from time to time. It is, therefore, important to realise that your approach to skiing should . . .

1. make use of the advantages of modern equipment, while avoiding potential disadvantages in some areas,

2. be based upon movements related to the human frame and your own in particular,

3. be based upon the principles which govern all movement and

4. take account of the reason *why* you are skiing and what you want to achieve at any particular time.

What is skill?

The word *skill* is used in many ways in everyday conversation and can mean different things to different people. In order to help you to develop *skilful skiing*, therefore, it will be helpful if I use 'skill' in a quite precise way.

We talk of the skill of doctors and tennis players, mathematicians and watchmakers. We hear of professional skills and gymnastic skills and, in industry, men are classified as skilled and semi-skilled.

All these uses have some essential factors in common, although some uses describe the ability of the person, i.e. the tradesman, the tennis player or the mathematician, while other uses describe complex or difficult tasks as skills.

For the purpose of this book and skiing, I propose to use the word 'skill' in the context of a person's ability, as evidenced by that person's actions, rather than in relation to the action itself.

For example, it is often said that dribbling in soccer is a *skill* but, for the purposes of this book, I contend that if someone barely able to dribble attempts to do so against active opposition, then what results is not likely to be a *skill*, it will be 'dribbling done badly'. It is the performance itself which will be more or less skilful and this will be judged as such only in the light of other performances under varying circumstances.

A parallel turn is not a skill, nor is throwing darts. Hitting the bull's-eye once and missing the board with many other throws is evidence of a fluke, not a skill, although hitting the bull's-eye repeatedly could be evidence of a dart-player's skill.

Allied to all uses of the word is the implication of experience and learning, quality and effectiveness with economy of effort and time.

I will, therefore, define a *skilful skier* as *one who sets realistic objectives and who has a learned ability to achieve them effectively, consistently and efficiently, under a wide range of environmental conditions.*

Skilful skiing in the high Alps

A skilful descent, with rucksack, off-piste

Skilful skiing

Technically competent skiers are often mistaken for skilful skiers, because of the characteristics of the movements they make. This is to mistake 'technique' for 'skill', a mistake which many ski schools and instructors have made and one which I hope to help you to avoid.

You will see from my definition above that skilful skiers have sound techniques, that is they are able to control their bodies and skis efficiently and consistently, but, more than sound technical ability, they have *sound judgement* too.

A skilful skier will have learned a wide variety of techniques to control himself and his equipment, and he or she will be aware of what his equipment will do for him, under a wide variety of circumstances.

He will recognise subtle changes and indicators in the snow, and will have learned what effects these are likely to have on his skis when he meets them.

The skilful skier must recognise subtle changes in the texture and nature of the snow and terrain

16

Sarah Lewis skiing extremely skilfully on the Lauberhorn

He will have a realistic assessment of his own ability and capabilities.

When a skier is aware of his total environment, when he sets himself testing yet achievable tasks and selects and adapts from his repertoire of learned movements those appropriate to his condition (emotional and physical) and to the terrain and snow conditions which enable him to achieve his aim efficiently, then he will be a *skilful skier* and will be recognised as such by his *skilful skiing*.

Skilful skiing is the result of learning, but not all learning will produce skilful performances. It is possible, indeed, quite easy in skiing terms, to learn many movements which are not efficient or effective and which may consistently interfere with sound performances. Such movement or position *habits* are to be avoided if possible, and to aid this process, you should always practise with an aim in mind, that is, whenever you are 'doing an exercise' or learning a new skiing manoeuvre you should always be aware of *why*. Both the short term and longer term reasons are important and if you don't know why you are doing something, what you are trying to achieve with your movements, then it is unlikely that you will develop a high level of skill.

○*Practise* with a purpose and be *aware* of your efficiency and effectiveness.

Only then will you become skilful.

Chapter two

A Route to Skilful Skiing

Skiing is done in mountains and on hills. It isn't done indoors where you are probably reading this book. But your route to skilful skiing can begin now. There are many ways in which you can prepare yourself **before you go.**

Can I be a skilful skier?

This is the first question you may ask yourself. After all, you may not have the right body-build to be a skier. A sprinter obviously has a different body-type from a marathon runner's, and if you are 5ft 5in and weigh nine stone, it is unlikely that you would ever be very successful at international 'putting the shot'.

Fortunately, skiing does not have any such built-in limitations and whatever shape or size you are, you will be able to harness the power supplied by gravity and use it skilfully through careful choice of objectives and terrain.

Equipment

As a keen skier, you will already have used skis and boots and may, indeed, have tried several models of each. It is normal and desirable to hire equipment as a beginner but as you progress, you will benefit from owning your own.

Models change from year to year and so I would recommend you to seek advice from a specialist ski shop, from your friends who ski and from an instructor or coach, before you buy.

When you go to buy your equipment be honest with yourself in assessing your skiing ability. Buy equipment suitable for your present ability. Don't be tempted to buy equipment suitable for the skier you intend to be, or hope to be, as this may actually interfere with your progress.

Ski boots

The most important item of your equipment is your pair of boots.

Boots serve several functions. They should protect your feet from the elements and keep them warm. They should support your feet in executing skiing manoeuvres and they attach you to your skis in conjunction with your bindings.

Your boots must fit well and be comfortable if you are to be able to transmit forces from your legs to your skis and, of course, be able to wear them all day, every day.

Points to consider When choosing your boots, consider each of the following parts of the boot.

1. The sole must conform to the D.I.N. specifications if it is to work efficiently in your bindings (ask in the shop).
2. Your ankle must be able to flex forwards easily. Many boots have hinges, in which case the hinge must coincide with your ankle flex. If it does not, firm inner soles may be used to effect this.
3. The boot should fit well around the ankle and move with the shin when you flex. Your shins may become bruised or chafed if the tongue is too hard or too loose.
4. The boot must be wide and long enough to allow your foot to spread out during skiing. It is a good idea to run around for a short while, *before* trying a boot on. A boot which is too narrow or too short will cause great pain in your arch and blisters on your toes, for, unlike ordinary shoes, modern ski boots will not 'give' with use.
5. The shape of the ankle cup and cuff must hold your heel down so that it cannot move sideways or more than 1 cm upwards.
6. The type of fastening system is not too important but bear in mind that if your boot has a built-in forward lean, it will be difficult to walk in and tiring to stand in, unless you can open the cuff and allow the lower leg to stand vertically to the floor.

The hinge at the ankle permits the boot to flex so that the shin can move freely forwards as shown by the arrows

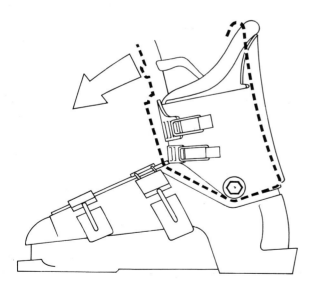

Ankle bend The amount of built-in 'forward lean' in your boot will vary from model to model. Slalom racers of an international standard (as opposed to good skiers who would like to become

international slalom racers) will use a high boot with limited flexing ability but with a high forward-lean angle. Such boots limit the range of movement, sensitivity and normal balance facility of *less* highly trained skiers and it is more important for aspiring racers to have easy forward flex, rather than a fixed built-in flex angle.

Skis

Your skis are the tools with which you will exercise your craft and develop your skill. You should know how they work.

Manufacturers now make several types of ski to suit different purposes and different types of skiing.

They can vary the characteristics of a ski by changing the materials from which it is made and by altering the relationships of the different parts of the ski, one to another.

Whatever its purpose, however, every ski has the same basic shape and its parts all serve the same basic functions. These parts are shown in the diagram.

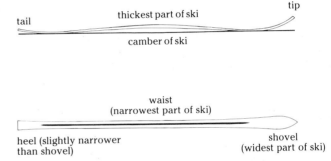

What the parts do The tip and tail of the ski turn up to permit easy sliding over and through the snow. Racing skis, especially Giant Slalom and Downhill skis, will have less turn-up at the tips to reduce air resistance at high speeds.

The *camber* of the ski causes your weight to be distributed along the entire contact length of the ski. This distribution is also affected by the flexibility of the ski and will affect the turning characteristics of the ski according to its flex pattern.

Flex pattern When you apply a force through your leg/boot to the centre of the ski and the ski resists at tip and tail, then the ski will distort into what is known as *reverse camber*. The shape of this reverse camber is a design feature of the ski and skis for different purposes will bend more easily in some parts than others.

Side cut All skis are waisted and because the wider parts of the ski are at the shovel and tail, these parts meet the most snow resistance when the ski is tilted onto its edge and a force is applied down the leg. As the ski presses into the snow, its flex pattern allows it to deform into *reverse camber*.

Carving If the snow supports the ski along its whole length and

Nic Fellows, All-England Junior Champion. Note the contrasting shapes of the pressured and non-pressured skis

20

the forces acting on the ski are mainly down the leg and at right angles to the lateral plane of the ski, then the ski will slide forward along its length which now lies in an arc—a banked track. Such an action is called *carving* and a turn made using this action is called a *carved turn*.

The shape of the arc will depend upon the type of ski (its flex pattern and length) and the weight and the speed of the skier. The variations in arc are, therefore, very limited with any single pair of skis, so only a very small number of turns in any descent down a mountain can possibly be carved turns.

Nevertheless, the *tendency* to carve is a very useful characteristic of modern skis and is used to enable very fine control to be exerted over a ski which has been deliberately skidded.

Torsional rigidity To put the ski in reverse camber, in order to turn, pressure must be applied through the leg and boot, more or less, sideways as well as downwards.

A ski which is longitudinally flexible but torsionally stiff will tend to carve, whereas a ski which has less torsional rigidity will tend to bend away from the area of greatest resistance which will be from the foot (where the force is applied) to the shovel (the widest part of the ski). That is to say, it will tend to grip and carve at the shovel and skid sideways at the heel.

Steering

This tendency to skid can be increased by rotating the leg (and hence the boot and ski) in the direction of the turn.

Sarah Lewis 'carves' a turn on her way to winning the Thomson Trophy Series (Girls) 1981

A ski's resistance to twisting shows its torsional rigidity (*above*); its resistance to bending shows its flexional rigidity, the opposite of flexibility (*below*)

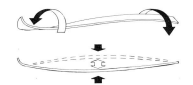

Boris Strel, bronze medallist in the 1982 World Championships, shows effective steering

Due to the momentum of the skier, when the ski, slightly edged,
is turned at even a small angle to its original line of travel, the
shovel will meet more snow resistance than any other part of the
ski and the ski will *tend* to rotate around this point.

The skilful skier will be able to use the shape, flex pattern and
torsional rigidity of his ski, in harmony with edge control, pressure
(against the ski) control and leg rotation, *to steer his ski very
accurately*, and will use more or less *skidding with a tendency to
carve* in order to permit turns of many and various radii at
whatever speeds he wishes to travel.

Selecting your skis

Local and current recommendations by people who know you and
the models of skis available are your best source of information
and, again, do go to a specialist ski shop for expert advice on
current models.

When selecting your skis, though, consider the design
characteristics and bear in mind the following general principles.

1. Racing skis are for *racing on*. Do not choose racing skis in
   order to impress, because unless you are physically and
   technically prepared to use them, they will only make life
   difficult.
2. 'De-tuned' competition skis, often called 'sport line', offer
   similar but less exacting characteristics.
3. 'Long' skis are faster with greater stability.
4. 'Short' skis turn more easily but offer less control at high speeds
   or on very hard snow.
5. Narrow skis grip well.

22

6. Wider skis tend to skid and, therefore, will begin to turn easily.
7. Soft flex skis with torsional rigidity will tend to carve.
8. Soft flex in the shovel area will enable turns to be started easily but may give rise to a tendency to skid thereafter. Such skis will also ride softly over undulations and give a smooth 'ride' in soft snow.

Tuning your skis

To give of their best your skis must be prepared and maintained.

Your skis (new ones included) will only work well if the following *fine tuning* has been done.

1. The sole and edges must be flat.
2. The edges must be square and free from burrs but rounded at tip and tail.
3. The sole must be clean and free from scratches. (These can be filled in with a variety of methods using polythene strips.)
4. The sole should be waxed to 'feed' the polythene and prevent it drying out.

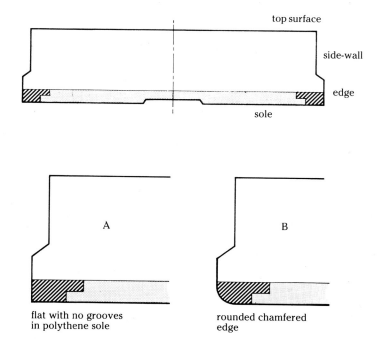

flat with no grooves
in polythene sole

rounded chamfered
edge

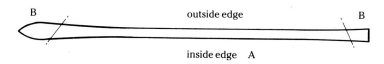

The sole of the ski must be flat in cross-section and at right angles to the side-walls. The edges must be square along the ski's length (A), but the ski will be easier to handle and turn easily (and yet will still grip when required) if the edges are chamfered at tip and tail (B)

23

Bindings

These devices are both *retention* and *release* mechanisms.

Modern, popular brand bindings all work to hold your boot in place, *retain* it when it is subjected to displacement forces and yet *release* it whenever those forces exceed a pre-set amount.

To work well they must be kept clean and free from dirt and grit and, to work at all, they must be fitted and adjusted to your individual requirements by an experienced and, indeed, qualified binding fitting expert.

Ski brakes

Modern bindings incorporate a spring-loaded 'prong' device which will stop your ski from running downhill if it should release in a fall.

If you intend to ski off-piste, use a retaining strap also, otherwise you may spend hours searching in deep snow for a lost ski after a fall.

Ski sticks

The simplest and yet often the most under-rated 'piece' of your equipment, ski sticks should have comfortable *handles* and may have straps or 'sword' grips.

They should have strong shafts and effective points, which will grip in ice as well as soft snow.

The baskets should be as light as possible and the sticks should feel light when you carry them in use.

Many postural and technical problems can arise in skiers using heavy sticks and, as it normally takes several weeks before your muscles are trained and 'fit' to carry your sticks well, it is important to have sticks which have their centre of gravity nearer to the handle than to the tip and which are as light as possible.

The length of your stick will affect the way you plant it and its effectiveness in pushing.

For normal recreational use and slalom racing, your sticks should enable the forearm to be horizontal when the stick is planted in the snow (elbow at 90°).

Downhill racers, who use their sticks for balance but who only plant them at the beginning of a race, may use longer sticks in order to get a better push off at the start.

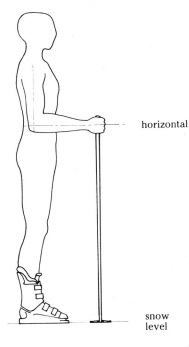

horizontal

snow level

Preparing yourself to ski

At the beginning of this chapter I said that whatever body type you are, you will be able to ski. Nevertheless there will still be a lot you can do to prepare yourself so that you are fit and ready to ski.

You can get yourself in the best frame of mind by reading skiing books and magazines, by watching films and by imagining or thinking yourself through your repertoire of skiing movements.

Mental training

Find a few minutes and a quiet place to lie down. Imagine the mountains:

- a specific mountain, on a fine, crisp winter's day.
- imagine yourself stepping out of the cable car, or getting off the chair lift.
- visualise yourself putting your skis on, now your sticks, goggles or glasses in place, zip up your collar,
- visualise all the little details,
- and then set off down a well-known run, 'feel' the sensations of the movements, the pressures against the soles of your feet, the wind on your face,
- watch the terrain and the snow texture as it comes towards you,
- slow down and stop when you feel your legs becoming tired through continuous bending and stretching in the moguls.

Such mental *rehearsal* and visualisation can be very valuable and will prepare you well for your skilful skiing; but it will only take you part of the way.

To be completely prepared to make the most of your time on skis you must also prepare your body to be able to perform efficiently the tasks that you will demand of it.

Imagine your favourite mountain on a fine, crisp winter's day

25

Chapter three

Body Preparation

I have deliberately chosen not to call this chapter *fitness training* as that involves other factors which are covered elsewhere in the book.

Fitness often means different things to different people but in a sporting context it is used to mean 'fitted' for the task, 'in suitable condition for . . .' or 'ready for . . .'

The implications are that:
1. it is achieved *prior* to participation and
2. that it is specific to the sport.

If, as a skier, you are *fit* then you are, by definition, *ready to ski.* This means that your body has been prepared to cope with the demands that your skiing will make on it, that you are able to ski (have learned some techniques which will enable you to ski) and that you have an appropriate attitude to skiing.

'Fitness' for skiing involves technical and 'mental' abilities as well as a suitably prepared physical condition.

It is this latter point that I wish to consider in this chapter—the physical condition of your body.

Let me begin by saying that if you can walk and run, you will be able to ski. Where and how you ski are different questions, of course!

It has often been said that 'skiing itself makes you fit' and, of course, this is true, but only if you ski at least every day for several weeks—and even then you will only become 'fit' for what you are doing. In order to learn *new* movements and to be able to cope with the new and *extra* demands that more advanced skiing will make of you, you must *prepare* your body beforehand.

It has also been said that because *skilful* movements are more efficient than less skilled moves, then 'fitness' is not so important as you become more skilful in your skiing. This is also true, but it is additionally true that as you become more skilful at what you are able to do now you are more likely to want to develop your skill and learn new techniques and apply them in new situations.

Some techniques, especially those whose movements are unfamiliar in 'normal' day-to-day activities, can only be learned efficiently and effectively (I am trying not to say 'correctly') if your body has been *prepared* beforehand.

Many skiers often have difficulty trying to learn new movements and quite often it is because they literally 'can't do it'. The body has not been suitably prepared and, therefore, is either very reluctant or totally unable to move in the prescribed manner. It may also be that they don't understand what is required, or that they are inhibited by their emotions, but these factors are discussed in Chapter Six. In any event, a suitably *prepared body* will enhance emotional disposition and movement awareness.

The aim of suitable body preparation is, therefore, to help you to achieve your full potential as a skier.

It has often been said that practice makes perfect, but it would be better to say that 'Practice makes perfect *only* if you are doing it well, developing it efficiently and repeating it often.'

Preparation of your body for skiing will:

1. Improve your *posture* and enhance your balancing ability.
2. Assist you to learn good quality movements which are not only efficient and effective *now* but will be most easily adapted to the demands of higher speeds and varied terrain.
3. Ensure that you can keep skiing for enjoyment, and practising the 'correct' movements longer, before *fatigue* forces these movements to change, or forces you to give up skiing for a rest.
4. Enable you to recover from fatigue earlier and thus enjoy more skiing with fewer aches and pains.
5. Reduce the probability of accidents caused by fatigue and, in addition, lessen the probability of injury where accidents do occur.
6. Improve your confidence and the acuity of your proprioception (through improved muscle tone) and as a consequence your enjoyment of your skiing will be enhanced.

Preparation of the body is based on the principle of growth and adaptation The body will *adapt* to cope with the stresses it meets in life (and training) and, as it *adapts*, it will grow, in addition to that growth which occurs in normal development during youth.

To be able to realise your full potential as a skier, your body must adapt in the following aspects of performance:

- *agility* and movement co-ordination
- *posture*
- *mobility*
- *general endurance* (stamina)
- *muscular endurance*
- *muscular power*
- *muscular strength*

It is important to recognise where you are at present, before you begin your journey of body preparation.

This reminds me of the old joke about the tourist who enquired of a local resident which was the best route to a particular beauty spot.

'Let me think now,' said the local, 'the best route to . . . eh? Well, I'm not too sure, but I can tell you this, it doesn't start from here!'

And so it is with *growth* and *adaptation*. It doesn't start from here and now. Your body began to grow and adapt from an extremely early age. The process has already begun.

Good basic posture, confidence and fitness enable Paul Hourmont to enter a slalom turn in good balance, lose balance momentarily and then regain it again very quickly, going on to win this run of the British Junior Championship's slalom

Ideal body preparation

This will begin at a very early age and essential growth is, of course, determined genetically, but appropriate diet and exercise will contribute to the growth of a healthy body.

Preparation for sport and all aspects of living should take place at the *appropriate time* in the growth of the child/adult if *full* potential is to be realised. This means that some forms of training and, therefore, adaptation are more appropriate at certain periods of our growth and development than at others.

From the moment of conception the body begins to grow. It *adapts* within the capability of its genetic endowment according to its environment. *Champions are both 'born' and adapted.*

The *ideal preparation* for skiing can be seen to have three distinct phases:

1. The *foundation training* phase.
2. The *preparation* (specific) phase.
3. The high-performance *competition* phase.

Each of these phases must take account of the natural growth and development of the skier if his/her greatest potential is to be realised, in safety and health, without damage to the skier.

As you are now old enough to read and afford to go skiing, it is, sad to say, too late for you ever to reach the greatest potential that you had when you were born. But you can, nevertheless, reach your highest potential from here, by complete preparation beginning with phase 1. Unless, of course, you had an ideal foundation training, in which case you will already be recognised as intelligent, agile, powerful, well adapted and very capable in many different sports.

Foundation training

This begins *ideally* when you are very young but may begin at any age. It gives the vitally important *base* on which *all future* development will depend.

The emphasis should be on play, enjoyment, variety and versatility, with a wide range of actions in many environments.

It is concerned with balance, agility, co-ordination of movements, confidence and experience and sensory meaning. *Foundation training* should enhance the natural development of the nervous system and the body's system for *neuro-muscular control.*

Foundation training should also improve the health and efficiency of the body's respiration and circulatory systems.

Foundation training should maintain and enhance the mobility that all young children have.

Foundation training occurs ideally between infancy and puberty. It should enhance and develop:

○ *agility* and co-ordination of movement with sensory input.
○ good *posture*, for balance and control
○ good *mobility* for flexible and extensive movements

An England squad junior during extended foundation training

○ efficient cardio-vascular-respiratory systems (for *stamina*)
○ sound patterns of movement for *basic techniques*.

Preparation training
This will be the major form of training for most skiers and is designed to build on foundation training in order to enhance the adaptation of a growing body to skiing.

The emphasis will be on specific training for skiing but a significant proportion of activity time should still be spent on other sports and physical activities.

Preparation training will overlap with foundation training and for ideal development will begin before puberty.

Care must be taken at this age to ensure that only exercise appropriate to the growth and development of the skier is undertaken.

This means that specific stressing of the body's systems must only use 'normal and natural' work.

Weight training must *not* be introduced until after puberty and only very light weights must then be used, in order to learn the 'correct' techniques, until after the growth of the long bones (legs and arms) has ceased and the cartilage at the joints has begun to harden.

The introduction of weights while the body is still growing can result in chronic injury, especially to the knees and spinal column. *Preparation training*, then, begins when interest in skiing makes it a 'first choice' sport. It should:

enhance:

    co-ordination,
    good *posture*,
    good *mobility*,

and further develop:

    general endurance (stamina)
    muscular endurance,

and then after puberty, develop:

    muscular power,
    muscular strength.

High-performance competition training
This will normally occur during the post-pubescent period and early adulthood.

It is specifically designed training, to enable an individual skier to achieve a peak of condition that will enable him or her to achieve the best performance possible—often in one specific competition, say, an Olympic games, or perhaps in a series such as the World Cup in one specific season.

This 'peak' of potential can only be reached if high-performance competition training is followed with total commitment, with strict targets and strict adherence to schedules. Such training will normally occupy over twenty hours per week and will only ever

Dennis Edwards, of the English and British squads, measures his leg-power with a sarjent jump

Ingemar Stenmark, the world's most technically precise skier, on his way to the gold medal and World Championship, 1982

29

be fully effective if sound foundation and extensive preparation training have been followed.

High-performance competition training will embrace tactical, technical and 'psychological' training in addition to body preparation and is, in the main, outside the scope of this book.

The development of your skilful skiing will be based upon the quality of your foundation and preparation training.

In the remaining section of this chapter we will consider those aspects of your *foundation training* which may have been inadequate, and then consider your *preparation training*.

Preparation of your body for skiing

It is important to remember the basic principle of growth and *adaptation*. Adaptation is a continuing process. Your body will adapt (eventually) to the situation it finds itself in—even sedentary situations. In fact, it *adapts* to doing very little exercise, quite easily.

Your body was designed to function at its best, however, when it is being exercised. To continue to improve in systemic, structural and functional health and to enable it to adapt its growth and function so that it is prepared for skiing, you must exercise *regularly* and *often*.

You will see one-page 'fitness training schedules' in leaflets and 'short courses' in booklets. These are all right if you follow them *every* day. There is no short cut to 'fitness'. *Body preparation* cannot be achieved in three weeks before you go on holiday, it is a way of life.

Whether you intended it or not, what you did when you were young has partially determined what condition you are in now. How you live *now* will determine how *prepared* you are to ski in the future.

Preparation training is a *way of life:*
  'a little every day'
In order to become a skilful skier, you must attend to *four* areas from your *foundation* training as an important part of your specific *preparation* for skiing.

These vital areas are:
  ○Agility ○Posture ○Mobility ○Stamina

A. Agility

The quality of your co-ordination and your agility can be enhanced if you can find time, at least twice per week, to play a game which involves quick movements and interaction with other people or equipment.

Of special value will be:
Dancing, either ballroom or disco, soccer, squash, tennis, volleyball, etc. These will also be useful in developing your general *endurance*. Whatever your age, and especially if you are over 35 years of age, remember to begin all exercise *gently* and

increase slowly.

Allow your body to *adapt*, slowly but surely.

B. Posture

Improve your posture and you will improve your skiing.

Poor posture seems to be a modern ailment. Round shoulders, flat chest and flabby abdomen are the rule rather than the exception.

Good posture arises in the lower back and spreads downwards to the legs through the pelvis and upwards to the head, through the spine and shoulder girdle.

Good posture depends upon good muscle tone in the *centre of your body* and the following exercises will help you develop just such muscle tone and improve your posture.

Posture exercises

1.1 Lie on your back, on the floor. Feel the hollow in the small of your back.

Skiing with such a hollow back causes stiffness, awkwardness and ineffective angulation and rotation of the legs.

2 Roll your pelvis around and upwards until you feel your lower back pressing lightly on the floor.

3 Now try to relax your abdominal muscles and still keep your lower back on the floor.

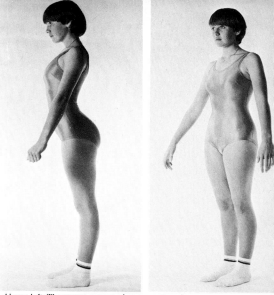

2.1 Lie on your back, with your legs 'tucked up'.

2 Feel your lower back touching the floor.

3 Slowly straighten your legs out horizontally and keep your back on the floor.

Above left: The worst aspect of poor posture is poor muscle tone in the abdomen and hence a hollow spine

Above right: Philippa shows improved posture by rotating her pelvis upwards, and thus straightening her lower spine with improved abdominal muscle tone

Poor posture with a hollow back prevents many skiers from progressing beyond elementary turns

Powerful leg steering with effective angulation requires good basic posture

3.1 Move onto your hands and knees.
  2 Push your tummy down towards the floor and hollow your back.
  3 Lift the small of your back and feel your pelvis tilt.

Exercise 3

Try to keep your back straight when you do this exercise (4)

4.1 Sit with your hands behind you, facing forward and with your legs bent.
  2 Bend your elbows, raise your feet, straighten your legs and hold them still.
  3 Straighten your back and hold your tummy in.
5.1 Kneel down with your thighs nearly upright.
  2 Hollow your back and keep your shoulders vertically above your hips and feel how your pelvis tilts downwards (at the front).
  3 Tilt your *pelvis* upwards, by drawing your abdomen upwards and inwards.

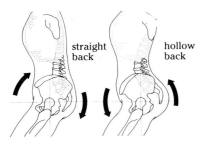

straight back

hollow back

pelvis tilted upwards

pelvis tilted downwards

6. Practise the above exercises standing upright.
7. Endeavour to incorporate the 'pelvic tilt' into all your daily movements, sitting down and standing as well as walking and, of course, skiing.

A hollow back 'separates' the lower from the upper body. People often appear to have knock knees, or bow legs, awkward arms and, indeed, flat feet *along* with a hollow back.

The pelvic tilt in good posture underpins all harmonious movements and is a condition to be mastered *now* if it was not developed in your foundation training.

Note how Philippa's elbows bend and pull backwards—this often accompanies a poorly tilted pelvis in skiers who have poor posture and poor dynamic balance

◄Boris Strel, bronze medallist in the 1982 World Championships and World Cup winner (Cortina), has an excellent pelvic tilt

C. Mobility

Good mobility aids agility and reduces the risk of injury. Mobility is the measure of the range of motion in a joint. Skilful skiing demands a good range of movement in the hips. In addition, an increase in the range of movement in your shoulders, back, and knees (being able to straighten them whilst hips are flexed) will improve your confidence and reduce the probability of injury in a fall.

Mobility exercises Exercises for developing the flexibility of your muscles (increasing your joint mobility) should be done twice per day, once at the beginning of the day, before a training session, and once again at the end of training.

Stretching exercises before training will help to prevent injury and also improve the ability of muscles both to contract and to relax.

Stretching after training helps to prevent muscle soreness and will serve to *maintain* the mobility achieved in previous stretching, as muscles tend to shorten in strength and endurance training.

Important note The skiers illustrating the exercises are dressed

Sarah Lewis shows a good pelvic tilt which enables her to angulate efficiently and effectively

This skier cannot angulate efficiently because his pelvis is tilted downwards instead of upwards, as can be seen in his hollow back and 'hip out'

During training and at races, Nic often has to do his stretching exercises in the confined space of a hotel bedroom

lightly, in order to show you all aspects of the movements and shapes. It is *very important* that when you do these exercises in your daily routine you are warmly dressed. You must wear at least a training suit and, for preference, long socks over the knees and a shirt or sweater as well.

You must be very warm when you are stretching.

The method you must use to stretch your muscles is known as *static stretching*. It is possible to stretch by bouncing or by being pushed but these methods may tear your muscles and can be harmful.

If one muscle group is particularly stiff or short, spend more time there. Stretching must not be hurried.

Stretching exercises
When you are stretching it is important to concentrate your attention on the sensations in the muscles. Try to *relax* the muscles under stretch *and* the muscles on the other side of the joint. For example, when stretching the hamstrings, try at the same time to relax the quadriceps on the front of the leg.

1. Hamstring stretch Crouch down and put your hands flat on the floor.

Slowly straighten your legs, keeping your palms on the floor.

In each exercise, move to the maximum extent of the joint's range. Hold that position for seven or eight seconds and try to relax. You will find you can now extend the joint further—stretch your muscles slightly. *Gently press* and *hold it* for around ten seconds. Repeat this two or three times.

2. Hip stretch Sit on the floor, legs astride and straight, arms out to the sides.

Slowly bend forward at the hips, keeping your back straight, and try to touch your chest or abdomen on the floor.

3. Frontal stretch Lie on your stomach. Place your hands beside your shoulders and then push upwards, take your head back and keep your hips on the floor.

Initially you may have to bend your back, but try to keep it straight and bend from your hips

Fiona Pulsford, English squad member, demonstrates the frontal stretch

34

4. The bridge Lie on your back. Place your hands 'overarm' by your shoulders and lift yourself into a bridge or 'crab'. Try to straighten your legs.

If you have a history of back problems do not do any exercises which arch your back totally. The exercises for posture involving the pelvic tilt should, however, be beneficial. If your back complaint is either chronic or serious, you should consult your doctor.

5. Hurdle stretch Sit on the floor in a 'hurdling' position. Try to place your thighs at right angles. If you can manage this, slowly bend forward from hips.

6. Shoulder stretch Sit on the floor, hands pointing backwards, slide your hips towards your feet, keeping your hands flat on the floor.

Philippa shows an excellent bridge

Hurdle stretch

Shoulder stretch

Shoulder and upper back stretch

Philippa shows excellent hip flexibility

7. Shoulder and upper back stretch Kneel down and slide your palms along the floor. Keep your hips high and press your chest and shoulders down towards the floor. Keep your arms straight.

8. Hip stretch Sit on the floor and pull your feet in towards you. Hold on to your feet and press your knees towards the floor.

In this exercise, the coach resists Philippa as she presses backwards; she *then relaxes* her back muscles and pulls her tummy closer to the floor

9. Hip stretch You may sometimes see a coach or partner *appearing* to push against the back of a person stretching.

What is happening is that the person doing the stretching bends as far as possible and the partner *holds* her/him in this position, whilst she pushes *back* against the partner and then relaxes and stretches further. The partner may follow and repeat.

The partner must *not push* against the skier at all, ever!

10. The splits You should work up to this with other hip-stretching exercises. When you can do it, keep practising it to both sides to maintain your hip mobility.

Lateral splits

Alternate this exercise with left leg, then right leg, forward

Ankles; *dorsi* and *plantar* flexion

11. Ankle flexing This helps to stretch both the Achilles tendons and the anterior tibialis, the muscles on top of your ankle.

Sit upright with your legs straight.

Pull your toes right back towards you.

Push them away from you and point them.

36

D. Stamina

This fourth part of your foundation training will ensure that you have a basic level of general endurance which will enable you to train at all other aspects of skiing and preparation training for longer periods than would otherwise be possible.

This is best achieved by training your *aerobic system*—your heart and oxygen transport system.

You will achieve a good training effect by working your whole body submaximally (heart rate 120–180 bpm) for periods of three minutes or more.

You can start off by vigorous walking; later, running or cycling, skipping or swimming will all help to improve your aerobic capacity for work.

Another aspect of general endurance, very appropriate to skiing, is your *anaerobic system*. This can be trained by working at maximum effort for about one minute (heart rate 160–180+ bpm).

Interval sprinting is a good way of increasing your *anaerobic capacity*.

Interval sprinting You should run, skip or ride for 30–60 seconds flat out, eight or ten times in a set. Let your pulse drop to 150 bpm in between repetitions and then to 120 bpm between sets. Do three sets.

Interchange your interval running with cycling and skipping for variety and with aerobic work for a change (as good as a rest!).

Preparation training

In addition to your foundation training which you *must do* if you are to become a skilful skier, you will also benefit from more specific training in muscular efficiency.

The most important aspects of *muscular efficiency* required for skiing are:

Power and muscular endurance

Power is best defined as the rate of work. It is dependent upon your strength and the *speed* with which you can *apply your strength*.

Power training This is a specific form of training and involves working against resistance and doing so quickly. If you have finished growing you may begin power training using weights, either on bars or on machines, as installed in many gyms these days.

If you have not finished growing yet, concentrate on endurance training and *do not* use any weights in your training.

Exercises The following are examples of exercises you may do for power training, but for specific exercises and schedules you should consult your coach.

Muscular endurance This is the ability of the muscles to contract vigorously and continuously, against moderate resistances.

It is best achieved by bicycling and circuit training.

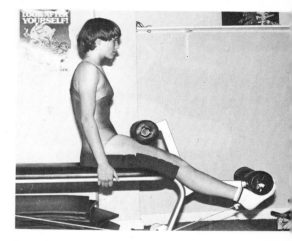

Gymnasium equipment can aid power training. Resistance from the machines, in this case against the extension of the legs, must only be raised under the supervision of a good coach. If you are still growing taller, do not do these exercises or any others using weights

Strong chest and shoulder muscles are important in skiing. They enable your stick control to be accurate

37

Back lift: Lie face down and then lift up as high and as quickly as possible

You may train for muscular endurance without weights if you have not finished growing and it will have a positive effect on your power output also. If you have finished growing you may use light or moderate weights, doing up to thirty repetitions.

The following exercises done in a 'circuit' will, however, usually be the most convenient.

1. Back lift.
2. Sit-ups or 'V' sits.
3. 'Windscreen Wipers'.
4. Push-ups.
5. Lateral jumps.

The use of 'home gym' apparatus such as a simple 'resistance expander' can also be useful for shoulder exercises, bicep curls and leg adduction and rotation exercises.

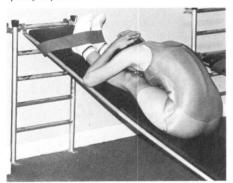

Sit-ups: as your endurance and power improves, you should incline your legs upwards

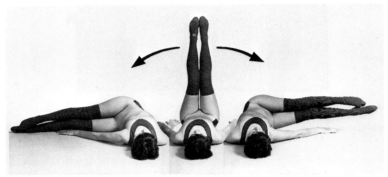

'Windscreen Wipers'

Push-ups: Do not lie on the floor, but first lift your hips off the floor; then, keeping the body straight, push up to straight arms. Lower with control, and *just touch* the floor with your chest

As your condition improves, you will need to consult more specialist books on preparation and high-performance competition training or, better still, work with a coach who knows your needs and who will prepare your schedule for you.

Whether you work with a coach or alone with friends,

remember that your foundation and preparation training must be a regular part of your life if it is to be effective.

Training schedule

Each week you should find time to do exercises for your *posture*, preferably once a day for five minutes.

Do your endurance work at least fifteen minutes every other day and circuit training, for ten minutes or so, again every other day.

Ten minutes of mobility exercises each day, before and after your endurance work or circuit training, is equally—if not more—important.

Keep up your mobility exercises throughout the year—twice a day! As you approach the skiing season, change from general endurance to muscular endurance exercises and, if you have finished growing, add power training to your muscular endurance training a month or so before you first go skiing.

This means that, in total, you must be prepared to spend a minimum of 25–30 minutes each day in *body preparation*—time well spent, as you will realise immediately you put your skis on again.

Stand with good skiing posture, and then jump, laterally, from outer foot to outer foot

'Home Gym' apparatus such as this powerful 'Resistance elastic rope' is not usually as good as gymnasium apparatus, but is useful if you need to exercise at home. In this exercise I am strengthening my leg rotators and adductors—muscles used in every ski turn, but hard to train on conventional equipment

Chapter four

At the Ski Centre

As a keen skier, you probably manage to get away to the snows of the Alps or Scotland at least once every year, but is this enough? Can you expect to become a very skilful skier unless you spend more time on skis?

Thorough physical preparation will ensure that you can make the most of the time you spend on skis and later chapters will guide you through your movements, but expertise will come sooner if you can ski regularly.

Dry ski slopes

Developed in the 1960s as a learning aid for beginners, dry ski centres have changed and grown over the years and a large number of ski centres all over Britain now enable keen skiers to practise their sport.

Young racers can now train relatively locally and competitions of national and international standard are held regularly throughout the year.

More than half of the current British Olympic ski team did their early training on dry ski slopes and I recommend them to all keen skiers who wish to improve.

Konrad Bartelski, Britain's best-ever downhill ski racer, skiing slalom at Gloucester Ski Centre

A local ski club

When you began skiing, in a ski school class, the class members gave each other support and encouragement, and you will discover this at your local ski club—contact the English Ski Council, Scottish National Ski Council, Ski Council of Wales, or Ulster Ski Federation for addresses of your local clubs which will have access to dry-slope skiing or skiing on local snow when it falls (with the use of a club ski lift), or both.

Coaching

This is a word in common use in most sports, yet it has only recently begun to appear in the skiing world.

Coaching is fundamentally different from instruction in several ways, but the most important differences can have a profound effect on you if you are aware of them.

Ski instruction, in practice, is designed to introduce non-skiers into skiing and where it is given through organised ski schools it reflects the 'product' that the school is trying to sell.

Coaching on the other hand is not readily available through ski schools and is only beginning to emerge in ski clubs.

Ski instructors are trained to teach skiers when they are on holiday, for one week or two. In Continental ski resorts, for example, ski instructors spend most of their time teaching foreign holidaymakers how to ski. Who teaches the locals? Why do different ski schools teach different methods, yet the champion skiers from every country all ski in pretty much the same way?

The answer lies in the fact that keen skiers, in all countries, need more than ski instruction once a year, they need help all the time—they need coaching.

A coach will work, usually through a club, with one or several skiers over many years. He or she will oversee the skiers' development in total terms. The coach will have a supportive and caring relationship with skiers and will know each individual personally, working with them for *long-term* results.

Swiss and Austrian coaches work with Swiss and Austrians locally and it is, therefore, very unlikely that you will ever come across one when you are on holiday.

Since its formation in 1979, the English Ski Council has recognised this problem and is now training coaches. Many clubs in Britain already have the services of coaches available to their members and many artificial ski centres can offer *coaching* to regular, keen skiers, in addition to the *ski instruction* which is available for newcomers to the sport.

In some respects, it is not important whether people are called instructors or coaches; what is important is that in your search for skilful skiing, in your pursuit of personal excellence, you need to have a long-term view and develop your skiing steadily and continuously, with physical, technical and other developments taking place in harmony with each other.

The following chapters will help you to view your skiing through the eyes of a coach. You will be able to work on the fundamental factors which determine the level of your skill, ignoring the commercially popular product, which is often arbitrarily emphasised out of all proportion to its worth.

This process will be enhanced if you join your local ski club and if you start skiing regularly at a good dry ski centre.

The holiday resort

What you do when you arrive at your holiday resort will depend upon your ability and experience. You will be fortunate if you are with a small group of friends of a similar standard, enthusiasm and commitment.

If you have been snow skiing once or twice before, join the ski school, at least for your first few days. This way you will adjust to the snow, the altitude and the mountain environment in safety and use the expertise of the locals to show you the layout and the possibilities of the ski area.

You may have been skiing for several years and training regularly on a good artificial ski slope, in which case you may not wish to join the ski school. You will benefit from skiing in a small group and working positively on your skiing, concentrating on specific areas that have been recently mastered in training.

It is possible that you have been able to go on a club holiday where your coach is accompanying you, in which case you need very little further help from me. But if you are not so fortunate then I suggest that you do have some instruction while you are in the resort, preferably after two or three days and for periods of an hour or so spread out over three or four days.

Private instruction, in a small group, with a good instructor (who may, if you are lucky, be a coach in the local ski club) will serve you well.

Evaluate your instructor

Evaluate your instructor and change him if you are not improving or enjoying yourself.

Ultimately, you will be better off skiing with your own small group of friends than with a bad ski instructor.

Hopefully, however, you will find a good ski instructor; he is likely to be qualified (many ski schools employ non-qualified skiers as instructors over the busy periods, so beware) and he will have his name and photo listed in the ski school office. Take an interest in him as a person, not only as a skier, and above all, remember that he is an expert 'watcher'. He will see the 'real you' and be able to assess your strong and weak areas, so you needn't try to impress him. If he lives in the Alps, he has seen the world's best skiing—your ability won't impress him a great deal, but your progress and your attitude will.

Tell him what you can do and what sort of terrain you can cope with, *modestly* and precisely, and watch *everything* he does, not only the way he demonstrates but even how he gets on the ski lift or carries his skis.

You can learn a lot by watching.

The good instructor

○ will be polite, introduce himself and learn your name, and will chat to find out about you as a person.

○ will evaluate your skiing and your aspirations.

○ will take care to ensure that you understand 'what *and why*' in his lesson.

○ will praise your effort and your successes.

○ will demonstrate how he expects you to attempt the movements—now.

○ will choose the terrain very carefully, and tell you or show you why.

○ will sometimes ski behind you and comment on your choice of pathway as well as your technique.

○ will keep you moving at a useful rate, while he does a lot of watching.

○ will care about you enjoying yourself and improving your skiing.

○ will ensure that you get to the end of the run(s) safely.

The poor instructor

○ will be arrogant and give you the impression that he is doing you a great favour by skiing with you.

○ will teach you to ski 'his' way without regard to your past experiences, or your wishes.

○ will find faults in all your movements.

○ will show how you could hope to ski in five years' time.

○ will ski ahead, saying only 'follow me'.

○ will take you (fast) down difficult terrain to show you how good he is.

○ will keep you standing still, while he does all the demonstrating (and talking) and you do all the watching.

○ will care that you think he is good and wonder what the other instructors on the hill think he looks like.

○ will ensure that he leaves you—on the dot—at the end of the lesson period.

Addresses of the UK governing bodies

For further information about:
    Competitions,
    Personal performance award schemes,
    Courses for instructors, coaches and competition officials,
    Local facilities
and
    Local ski clubs,
contact your governing body:

In England: The English Ski Council
                Area Library Building
                The Precinct
                Halesowen
                West Midlands B63 4AJ
                Tel: 021-501 2314

In Scotland: The Scottish National Ski Council
                110a Maxwell Avenue
                Bearsden
                Glasgow G61 1HU
                Tel: 041-943 0760

In Wales: The Ski Council of Wales
                Tal y Bont
                Ffestiniog
                Gwynedd LL41 4HG

In Ulster: The Ulster Ski Council
                16 Upper Green
                Dunmurry
                Belfast BT17 0EL

When you are skiing you are learning—learning what you are doing. You may not intend it, you may not even be aware of it, but your body will be changing slightly as a result of your skiing experiences and so, if you want to develop skilful skiing, you must take some responsibility for your own learning and become aware of what is happening when you are skiing.

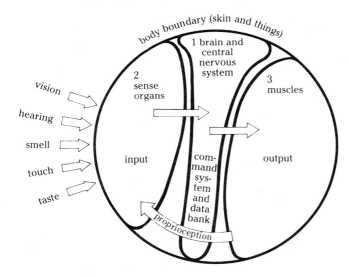

What is learning?

Psychologists believe that *learning* is related to internal neural changes which enable new behaviour to emerge, with a certain level of permanency. No one is totally sure how learning takes place, but I shall work from a model which will help you to appreciate what is happening to you when you are skiing.

When you begin to ski, the decision to do so, where, when and why, etc., has been made within the body.

Your six senses

The sense organs are constantly receiving information, from touch, taste, smell, vision, hearing and proprioception. The first five senses you will know all about, but the sixth sense, your 'internal' sense, may not be so familiar.

Proprioception is a sensory system which monitors, through sense receptors in the joints and muscles, where all your body parts are, what positions they are in relative to each other, and what degree of tension or movement is in the muscles. It is the sense which allows you to touch the end of your nose with your finger, with your eyes closed.

The semi-circular canals in your ears, which sense if your head is upright or moving, are also part of your proprioceptive sensory apparatus.

Your sixth sense is very real and very important in skiing, but more of that later.

Perception

All the senses feed information (*input*) into the brain and central nervous system—*all the time*. If the brain were to 'listen' to all of it all the time, it is likely that the brain would sense chaos.

This would not be very useful, so in this model I suggest that the brain *selects* from the *sensory input* as a consequence of an internal *reference* system. It makes 'sense' out of the total amount of information by selection, reference and organisation, and this 'understanding' of the body's relationship with the outside world is called *perception*.

In terms of learning to ski, it is not too important what the real world or mountain is like; rather, what is of vital importance is what your *perception* of it is.

You will bring to your percepts memories of fears, joy, exhilaration and other emotions which are drawn from your past experience and which do not exist outside your body, but which will form part of your *perception* of the *outside world* and your relationship with it.

Action

Following the process of selection and interpretation of the sensory input, your *perception* will cause the central nervous system to effect action in your muscles (*output*). *Your body will move!* The muscles, controlled from your nervous system, will enable the body to interact with the outside world.

As soon as you begin, and as you continue to move (to ski), the information which your senses receive changes.

Your perception of movement will be based upon input from all six senses, although taste and smell are probably not significant.

The pressure touch against your feet and shins, the sound of the ski in the snow, the feeling of the wind on your face and your vision will all be collated with your proprioceptive sense of internal movement to give you an overall perception of *movement* called *kinaesthesis*.

Your kinaesthetic perception is your major *feedback* loop which not only regulates your movement but is in itself a major source of pleasure in skiing.

The use of stretch materials in 'contour fit' clothing for gymnasts and skiers enhances kinaesthesis by increasing the sensory information about the muscle tone and body shapes/movements through the increased area of touch against the tensioned membrane which encases the moving body

Feedback

Imagine yourself to be a guided missile, or a torpedo. You decide on your 'target'. Select a realistic one, according to your perception of the hillside and your current ability. It may be to ski a slalom course if you are a trained racer, to descend part of a mogul field at a slow speed, or to attempt to link some skidded turns in a rhythmical manner. Set off in control and accept that *kinaesthesis* is your guidance system. Allow it to guide you to your target.

You will be amazed at how good your body is at controlling itself, provided you have selected a 'target' that you *can* hit and have built the torpedo (trained your body) so that it has the means to reach the target.

Difficulties arise when you *either* select a target which is out of your range *or* try to interfere with the control and guidance system, consciously, en route.

The recipe for a successful descent, therefore, is

1. Think before you set off.
2. 'Survey' the hillside and yourself.
3. Select a reasonable task (target).
4. Set off—do not *think*.
5. Develop your awareness of what you are doing and what is

happening, and this awareness, your *kinaesthetic perception*, will guide you to your target.

Of course, you may be 'intercepted' en route, if the terrain turns out to be different from how you originally perceived it, for example, but in this case you will adjust your perception of the terrain and either change your way of skiing it, or change your 'target'. In either case you will *learn*.

If you pay attention to your sensations whilst skiing, *feel* what you are doing and are *aware* of what is happening, then your *perception* will become sharper and your control so much better. The manner in which you move will change as a result of the better-quality *feedback* your central nervous system and muscles are getting. Your skiing will change.

This model of skiing is very valuable because it shows how you can learn from small modifications of what you can do.

It is important to recognise where you *are*, *now*, because this is where you start from. It is pointless wishing you could ski in such and such a manner, wishing you could start from somewhere else; you cannot.

In your journey to skilful skiing, you start from *here*, *now*.

Change is implicit in learning and if the changes in your skiing are going to continue—and for the better—it will be because of changes that occur in one or other parts of the 'model' ...

... changes which you can influence if you are aware of the fundamental components of skilful skiing and how these relate to my 'model' of a skier.

Traditional ski schools and ski instructors concentrate largely on changing your *output*—your muscle movements—your 'techniques'. My model, however, shows you that any changes in your *perception*, your decision-making or your *emotions*, and in your *feedback* mechanisms, will cause changes in your *output*—your muscle actions—your body's movements.

The success of these small changes in your movements, related to your perceptions, will determine your rate of learning.

It is important to note that you will *learn* from what you *are* doing and not from what you wish to do, or hope to do! It is, therefore, important that each practice should be as successful and of as good a quality of movement as possible.

Think before you set off—set yourself a clear and realistic goal or target.

When you start moving, *don't think*; simply *be aware* of what you are *doing*.

When you reach your target, *evaluate* the results of your actions, and in this way you will *learn skilful skiing*.

Chapter six

Having set you a goal of improving your skiing so that it becomes increasingly skilful, having encouraged you to believe that you will be able to learn to do movements on skis that you cannot yet do, ski in places you cannot yet ski, and with an ease and control that you do not yet have, I must now indicate to you how you may achieve this.

In this chapter, I will cover the major areas which determine *skilful skiing* and in the following chapters look at details within each of these major areas, to which you can attend in your practising and which will contribute to improved quality, versatility, efficiency and control—in a word, improved *skill*.

As a skier, you live on a 'world' that is fundamentally different from the 'world' of non-skiers.

Non-skiers live on a *flat* *sticky* 'world' that is marked with *straight lines*, either parallel or at right angles to each other. *Muscles* provide power for *propulsion*.	Skiers, on the other hand, live on a *tilted* *very slippy* 'world' that is relatively *featureless*. Their motive power is supplied by *gravity*, *muscle* power being used to *steer* and *control* movements.

This means that the normal movements of non-skiers don't appear to work at first, partly because of the different mechanical factors, but mostly because of the difficulties in *orientation*. That is, understanding and 'reading' the terrain in relation to the movements that can be made on it. This 'sense' of strangeness will also cause excitement and anxiety, elation or fear.

To become a truly skilful skier, therefore, you must accommodate these new *sensations* and *feelings* and adapt your body movements to suit the new situation.

Skilful skiing has three major aspects. These are:
- ○ *perception*
- ○ *emotion*
- ○ *technique*

The extent of your skill as a skier will depend upon how well prepared you are for (good) decision making as your new, tilted, slippy, featureless and gravity-powered 'world' takes on form and then later, as this new 'world', the mountainside, becomes more complex and unfamiliar.

Skilful performances in different sports are recognised in several different ways. In some there is an emphasis on the *technique(s)*

Skilful Skiing

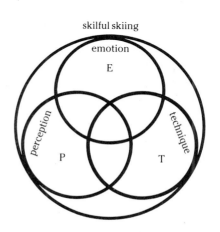

used, in others an emphasis on the *situation* and the demands that this makes on the performer.

Single technique in *constant* situation (closed)
　　e.g. athletics, bowling, shooting.

Multiple techniques in *constant* situation (closed)
　　e.g. gymnastics, dancing, skating.

Multiple techniques in *variable* situations (open)
　　e.g. team games, alpine skiing, slalom canoeing.

It can be seen, then, that skilful performances in sports are the use of *technique(s)* expressed in *closed* or *open situations*.
　Your skilfulness in skiing will, therefore, depend not only on your technical ability but on your ability to recognise the complexity of the situation you are in and, through learning, for this to become as familiar and as meaningful as possible.
　Thus, the *closed:open* nature of the situation will be partly inherent in the changing complexity of the mountainside, and partly in *your perception* of familiarity and order in the *variable* situations of an open mountainside.

The skilful skier will study and hence increase his understanding of mountains, weather, snow structures and terrain features, and will gain experience in interpreting these ever-changing conditions, at every possible opportunity

This racer's *perception* of the slalom course ahead (possibly the severely convex terrain) has obviously affected his *emotions* adversely. This, in turn, prevents him from making an appropriate *technical* response to the slalom course

The extent of your skilful skiing then will be a consequence of the quality and breadth of your *perception*, your emotional disposition and the quality, variety and appropriateness of the *techniques* which you 'select' to perform in the variable mountain environment.

There is continuous interaction between these three factors and development cannot occur in one without a profound effect on the other two and a consequent change in the level of skill in your performance.

For example: Your perception of a hillside will be affected by your own technical ability and, of course, your previous experience of similar conditions. What you decide to do on that hillside will be influenced by your emotions and will, in turn, influence your emotions when the decision is made. If, after commencing your descent, you perceive that the snow conditions are not what they seemed earlier, for example, ice lurks below a thin covering of powder snow, then your emotional disposition will change rapidly and the quality of your movements (your techniques) is likely to change as a consequence.

You will enhance your skill as a skier by attending to all of these areas in your training.

A further consideration will re-emphasise the importance of fitness training and body preparation.

A body which has become more powerful, with greater mobility and endurance, will permit new techniques to be learned and, more importantly in the short term, it will permit current techniques to be easily adapted to new environmental problems, and the awareness of this will be reflected in your emotional disposition, as your perception of yourself skiing the hillside changes during the descent.

All three factors are inter-dependent and interact continuously.

You must attend to all three factors if you are to increase your skill in skiing.

Building skill

Perception

This is the process of giving meaning to the information gathered by your senses. In order to improve the breadth and quality of your perceptual process you must attend to the information collected by your senses. In order to do this usefully as a training exercise, your emotions must not inhibit you, so you should perform familiar, habitual movements on easy terrain, to begin with.

Attend to the *sounds* of your skis on and in the snow—they will tell you a great deal about the surface you are skiing on.

Feel the different pressures that your skis exert against your feet, *feel* the different parts of your boots pressing on the corresponding parts of your feet and legs.

Be *aware* of the *shape* of your body and the *tensions* within it. Be aware of the different *parts* of your body as they move in relation to each other.

Smell the fragrance of the pine trees and the smoke from open log fires. Enjoy the sensations of moving in the mountains.

Watch the snow very carefully; note its texture by *looking* and *feeling*. You might even try exploring by taste as well. Different snow textures feel different on your tongue as well as in your hands, as well as under your skis.

Look for pathways in the snow—subtle changes of gradient, indicated by shadows or small changes in reflection. Look for indications of the nature of the terrain under the snow—walls and rivers are obvious but what of bushes and rivulets, stony fields or grassy slopes? The clues are there if you learn to see them.

Our perception is most acute when sensations are changing. However, changing sensations which are very familiar may become dull in our perceptions. After a while you may not 'hear' what the soles of your feet are telling you unless you 'listen' to them carefully.

Cultivate the habit of *awareness*—watch, listen and above all *feel* what is happening around you and inside you when you are skiing. The sensations will relate to each other, and your *perception* will grow richer and more valuable as a consequence.

When the terrain becomes more difficult you may find that 'things' are changing faster than you can cope with. Your senses are providing too much information for you to deal with—some sensations will begin to *interfere* with what you are doing.

In this case you must develop *selective attention*. Focus on *one* set of sensations only. In deep snow, for example, focus your *attention* on the pressure against the soles of your feet. Ignore all other sensations, until you find them impinging on your consciousness without any adverse effects.

Attend to the pressures under your feet

52

In moguls you may be upset by the *feeling* of hitting against the walls, and the *sound* of the ice as you skid out of control down the steep side of the mogul. The *sight* of another hundred yards of big, hard mounds which force you to bend and straighten your legs like an overworked piston may cause you to become defensive. Relax, enjoy the mogul field by focusing all your *attention* on to the soft, loose snow which lies in the hollows *between* the moguls. Ski the moguls in short sections, until you don't 'see' the bumps and ice any more, you see only the snow and the hollows—the pathways of other skiers—the skiers who made the moguls in the first place.

Alternative pathways through the troughs or hollows between and around moguls

Slalom courses consist of pairs of poles and flags (which can flutter in the wind and distract you). You must race between these poles in their pairs; you must choose a route, a pathway down the course.

A newcomer to slalom racing begins by seeing only a 'forest' of poles, and must find a pathway through them.

A valuable exercise for you when beginning racing is to ski through a random 'forest' of slalom poles in order to feel at home. Pathfinding, but in a situation where you cannot fail—every pathway works at this level.

Now try skiing the same 'forest' but making each turn similar in size and with the same rhythm as the previous turns. Your eyes will search for the appropriate *spaces between the poles* and you will find a pathway.

You will learn to ignore the poles which are not related to the rhythm of your movements and, in this way, you will be learning what the top slalom racers have learned, how to ignore the poles which don't affect you—to *attend* to the turning poles and the spaces between them.

Each young skier follows his or her own pathway through a forest of poles

53

In skilful skiing, you will use perception in several ways. Your perception of yourself and the mountain you are on will determine *where* you decide to ski, and *how* you attempt to do so.

When you are skiing your perception will act as a *feedback* loop to regulate what you are doing and so the quality of your skiing is directly related to the quality of your *awareness* of your movements and your pathway.

When you have stopped, your perception of what you have just achieved will affect how you proceed.

To make progress, be *aware* of what you are doing and *attend* to your good sensations—to your strong points.

Emotional disposition

Your emotional disposition at any moment will be a consequence of your *perception*. Emotions may have both positive and negative effects on your performance and it is, therefore, important to recognise your emotional disposition. By using the process of *selective attention*, you may effect an appropriate emotional disposition toward the goal you have set yourself, or, alternatively, you may change your 'goal' and so be able to continue to approach it with appropriate *emotional disposition*.

Speed which is perceived to be dangerous will produce anxiety. You should be able to attend to your control and stability or to the direction of your travel, say into a flat run out area, so that the (same) speed is no longer perceived as dangerous; anxiety is replaced by exhilaration or excitement.

Aggression can be valuable when tackling steep slopes or

Steep slopes must be tackled with positive, attacking movements making short sharp turns on a hard slope, but it can be counter-productive if soft and sensitive gliding is required for a smooth fast run. In this case, an awareness of your attitude, your emotional disposition, may enable a change to be made which will affect the nature of the movements made.

It is interesting to note that different emotional states are often reflected in different body shapes; anxiety will often cause a hollowing of the back, a pulling back of the shoulder blades and elbows and a stiffening of the legs.

◀ Skiers showing typical technical problems caused primarily through *anxiety*

Although this manifests itself as a postural or technical problem, in extreme cases it can only be cured by removing the cause of the anxiety. In less extreme cases an alteration in the posture, rounding the back, bending the legs and straightening the arms *forwards*, may well reduce the anxiety.

It is very valuable to be able to recognise your own emotions, and often those of your friends too, as you will perform at your best and learn most effectively only at very specific levels of emotional disposition.

To help you visualise this, the 'Yerkes–Dodson' arousal curve is most helpful.

Anxiety can often be controlled by trying to improve your posture; this young girl, although anxious, copes with her speed by pushing arms forward and bending her legs

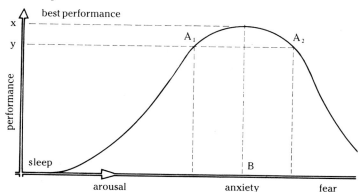

In reality, 'arousal' consists of many different factors. Each skier must identify which of these will raise or lower his/her body's overall arousal to produce optimal anxiety and activation (B) and hence the best performance (X). A somewhat less good performance (Y) will occur at two arousal levels, A_1 and A_2. Recognition of which one you are at will enable you to raise or lower your arousal level accordingly

55

Discretion is often the better part of valour

Emotional disposition is related directly to the level of activation of our bodies and our central nervous systems. This is known as our *arousal* level.

Our arousal level fluctuates on a spectrum from a very low level (sleep) to extremely high levels (intense excitement, hyperactivity, hysteria, 'petrified' with fear).

The diagram shows a relationship between our arousal level and our ability to produce a quality performance. Point B indicates the *optimum level of arousal* and this can be related to the *optimum anxiety* point on an emotional scale from boredom to fear.

You will ski at your best when you are appropriately aroused and 'anxious' and for easy tasks you may have to be 'psyched up' to perform well, but over-anxiety will 'psyche you out' and your performance will drop off.

If one can recognise where you are on your *arousal curve*, you can either 'warm up' or calm down in order to ski your best. This may mean simply warming up with exercises or calming down with quietness, or you may need to change your mind about what you are going to do.

On *easy* slopes, set yourself a precise task, something very specific, to be done accurately. On difficult slopes or difficult snow conditions, when you are well 'over the top of your curve', discretion is often the better part of valour.

You can recognise where you are on the curve by monitoring your own behaviour. At either end of the spectrum, boredom (and sleep) and great fear are easy to recognise. Areas either side of your optimum are not so easy.

Casualness, lack of attention to details and a slow heart rate are signs of low arousal; sweating, high heart rate, unusual over-attention to details, unusual amount of inconsequential chattering, hysterical laughter and jokes which you would normally consider 'silly' are all signs of too high an arousal level.

When you are at your *optimum arousal* you will feel yourself to be in a state of relaxed, *calm concentration*; you will probably have a hint of 'butterflies in the stomach' but you will feel very calm and your awareness of what you are doing and about to do will be very high. Your concentration will be easy.

Recognition of your emotions is vital if you are a serious competition skier, but very important, too, at all levels of ability, if you are going to be able to learn efficiently and perform skilfully.

An emotion/perception exercise You can investigate your emotional disposition while you are skiing with the following exercise. Find a steep, concave slope, with a longish run-out area. Set out down, making *linked* round turns.

When you judge that you can stop turning and start schussing *without* becoming frightened, do so—*schuss*.

During the schuss, ask yourself:

1. Are you frightened? If so, you judged wrongly.

2. If not, could you have started schussing earlier?

This 'test' will help you to discover your emotional threshold and improve the quality of your perception of yourself in relation to any particular skiing situation.

Techniques

Techniques are the *output* in skilful skiing, in terms of the 'model' in Chapter Five.

When the body moves, in order to achieve its aims in an activity such as skiing, it will tend to make patterns of movements which are more or less mechanically sound and which are repeated when similar results are desired in similar environmental conditions.

These movement patterns which are apparently regularly repeated are called ski techniques.

I say 'apparently' because in skilful skiing these patterns of movements are never *exactly* the same.

Many skiers learn techniques which they then reproduce identically during a descent, only to feel dissatisfied or frustrated. This is because it is unlikely that a *set pattern* of movement can ever be appropriate to the changing conditions of the body and changes in the snow and the terrain.

'Technique', then, is a convenient way of grouping together into one conceptual unit many small movements which combine into a larger recognisable pattern.

Snow plough turns, stem christies and compression turns are techniques, but although the general pattern of the movements which make up a compression turn will always occur in a similar sequence, the amount of 'edge', in relation to the amount of leg extension as well as to the speed of the movements and the radius of the turn on steep icy slopes and shallow, soft pistes, will always be different.

A major failing in many ski schools is that 'technique' is often taught for its own sake. Techniques can only be useful if they are *adaptable* to both the morphology of the skier and the variable conditions under which they will be used.

The author demonstrates compression turns

Your skill as a skier will be largely determined by the efficiency of your movements, that is, the quality of your techniques, but equally important will be the *adaptability* of your techniques and the *variety* of techniques that you can select at any given moment to solve your skiing 'problems'.

All ski schools and most skiing books demonstrate and teach discrete techniques. In a stem christie, for example, the skis will be stemmed in a set manner, closed at a given time and a standard body shape will be expected. This is fine for ski instructors' examinations but it hardly meets the needs of the real world—the open mountainside.

As your speed changes, as the snow resistance or the steepness of the hill changes, if your skis are long or short, soft or stiff, edges sharp or blunt, so the ingredients of your turn—your 'technique'—

Sarah displays versatility in coping with difficult
terrain problems

will need to be adjusted or varied in order to give you optimum
control.

In the following chapter I will consider the fundamental
constituents of all turning techniques and present them in such a
manner that you can investigate each in turn and then combine
them in an infinite variety of sequences and patterns, thus giving
you a continuum of technique which you can use *skilfully*.

In addition to turning, many other techniques will be used for
starting, stopping, accelerating, gliding, etc. and some of these will
be looked at in a later chapter, but control in skiing is gained by
turning and so the next chapter will concentrate on the use of
technique for this aspect of skilful skiing.

Chapter seven

Technique

A technique is a 'way of doing' something—*the manner in which you move your body* in order to achieve your goal or 'hit the target'.

Skiing techniques are movements of your body (and your equipment) which determine how you will move through the snow and down the hillside.

It is possible to move either efficiently or inefficiently, and therefore skiing 'techniques' may be either efficient or inefficient in respect of the movement itself in physiological, anatomical and mechnical terms.

Good-quality skiing will always be characterised by efficient movements—*good technique*. Skilful skiing is recognised as an *appropriate application* of good techniques (selected from your total repertoire) to the problems as *perceived* during a descent and which are influenced in that application by your *emotions*.

Ski techniques, then, are movement patterns which are technically sound. They will be a major part of any skilful performance.

Snow ploughing is a technique and is recognised by a general body shape and movements of the legs which cause the skis to skid forwards and sideways. The quality of the ploughing technique will depend on the efficiency of all the integral movements; good ploughing technique will always be appropriate to the terrain and the build of the skier, and will never be a fixed posture or movement *habit*—which, sadly, are too often learned in the ski schools which sell their own brand of technique.

Turning techniques

Commercial ski schools focus attention on turning techniques. This is quite reasonable, as turning is the most important means you have to control your descent.

Turning techniques are often given names, and such skiing turns are then characterised by their *differences*, for example plough turns, stem turns and parallel turns. These techniques, and the different ways in which they are performed, are often magnified and distorted in order to 'promote a brand image'—to sell the product. Different ski schools may teach turns with different emphases and you, 'the customer', can be forgiven for believing that one specific turning technique is superior to another.

As you become more skilful in your skiing you will, however, recognise the vital but subtle difference between *learning a turn* (a movement habit) and *learning how to turn* (sensitive movements performed in harmony with the terrain and your aims or 'target').

The skilful skier will recognise that all turning techniques are valuable and will be able to select and use different techniques from a wide repertoire, according to his target, his perception of the demands made by the terrain and his emotions and, in addition, he will be able to adapt his movements to changing demands during a descent.

The *highly* skilful skier, however, views turning techniques differently again.

The highly skilful skier recognises that all turning techniques are simply stages on a spectrum of movements which control the skis—a complete *continuum*. He recognises and utilises the *fundamental* factors that all turning techniques have in common, rather than the almost irrelevant details which differentiate them for the purpose of 'labelling' and 'product promotion'.

Your route to skilful skiing will be greatly shortened when you have had the chance to investigate—on the slope—these fundamental factors which determine control in *all* turning techniques.

Fundamental factors common to all turning techniques
All 'turns' on skis have a common objective—to change *direction of travel*.

The turning techniques employed, however, may be used to achieve, additionally, different objectives. Some may be used to turn and slow down or to turn and avoid obstacles, others to move with a pleasant rhythm which is both efficient and satisfying in itself—a source of pleasure—while others may be used to control the overall speed of descent and yet maintain an exciting speed of travel.

Whatever the reasons for turning on skis, the techniques used all have several factors in common.

In simple terms, to turn on skis, you simply point your feet (and, with good boots and bindings, thus your skis) where you want to go and then stay 'upright' while you go there.

This very simple statement is verified every time I see learners

The low mass of children's upper bodies allows them to explore many aspects of skiing without having great concern about their basic posture, which will improve as they grow

and experts skiing and, in particular, when a young child, who cannot 'decide' whether to point his skis where he wants to go—one at a time or both together, depending upon his ability to stay 'upright'—shows very clearly the 'obvious' way that a small body, unafraid but unco-ordinated as yet, will try to push his feet around and then worry about 'staying upright' later.

Skis may be 'pointed where you want to go' in many ways. One obvious way—in a plough turn—is to 'point them' in two directions at once, thus hedging your bets—keeping your options open, until you decide to reinforce one of the skis and then move towards the direction in which the reinforced (weighted) ski is pointing.

Another obvious way is to hop both skis simultaneously so that they land pointing in a new direction, towards that in which you want to go—the very basic parallel turn.

The fundamentals of turning techniques are those factors which will enable you:
○ to point your skis where you want to go
○ and then to go there
○ and to remain in balance above them.
There are **four fundamentals**, illustrated in the diagram.

The *quality* of your *turning technique* will be determined by the quality of your control and co-ordination of the *four fundamentals*, and the *type* of technique, the *name* of the turn if you like, will be determined by the *sequence* in which you begin the movements shown in the inner circles.

To become a truly skilful skier you must develop an awareness of *each* of these four fundamentals and improve your control and the quality of each.

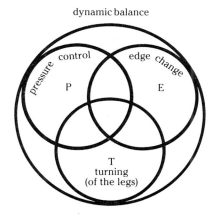

The four fundamentals:
Turning (of the skis)
Edge changing from one edge to another or from less edge to more edge, etc.
Pressure refers to the effect of your weight and momentum on or against your skis.
Dynamic balance balance whilst moving

In the first image (right) Sarah changes *pressure* from her left to her right ski. Note: her leg is rotated outwards. The second image shows an *edge* change with slight *rotation* of her leg. The third and fourth images show increased leg *turning* (medial rotation of the working leg) and *edging*—PET

Chapter eight

A Closer Look at the Four Fundamentals

In a 'static balance' mode the weight is carried through the heels

As all skiing requires good balance, the acquisition of *dynamic balance* is the highest priority. Sadly, this is often the most neglected part of skiing in many ski schools, so you must look closely at what is required before you begin to investigate the other three fundamental constituents of all turning techniques.

Dynamic balance

To understand and achieve good *dynamic balance* it will be helpful to compare it with *static balance*.

When your body is moving it behaves differently from when it is standing still. These differences can be seen in your posture and body shape, and also in the nature of the movements made to keep in balance.

When you are standing still or walking at slow speeds your body is upright and operates in a *static* or *responsive balance* mode.

Your feet are made of many small bones which form an arch. This arch carries your weight through its outer rim when you are standing still. Very often, the whole weight is carried through one foot at a time. The support leg will 'lock' straight and your centre of mass will be directly above your heel and the outside edge of your foot.

When walking, the outside edge of the heel of your foot will carry your weight as you place your foot ahead of you.

If you should need to *respond* to any unexpected forces disturbing your balance, 'ripples' of movement will occur at the *centre* of your body, in your hips and lower back, as well as in your arms and legs.

Your arms will normally lie close to your sides.

When you move at higher speeds, however, all this changes and your body will adopt a *dynamic* or *anticipatory balance* mode.

This balance mode differs from the static or responsive mode in several ways.

In order to cope with disturbing forces which are very likely to be met during movement, the body (and you) must *anticipate* the likely sources of such forces. Your eyes (and ears) must be alert and in a position to 'see ahead' with the greatest possible clarity of reference.

The shape of your body will also change in anticipation of distorting or disturbing forces.

The manner in which the feet work both to support and now guide your movements will change; the arms will move away from your sides and your *pelvis* should tilt in relation to your legs and spine in order to enable your muscles to work your 'lever systems' most effectively.

Dynamic balance mode differs from *static balance* mode in six major ways:

1. Your eyes must be alert and looking closely at the terrain ahead. *Eye line* should be *horizontal*.
2. The body *lowers*: leg joints flex—hips, knees, ankles.
3. The feeling of 'weight' moves forward of your heels. The *whole feet* support you and the front inside *edges* of your feet (the balls of the feet) are used to apply pressure for propulsion and control.
4. Your centre of mass will *not* be above your feet when you are turning and your *legs* will be *inclined inwards*.
5. Your arms will move out and forwards—you should *'hold a hoop'*.
6. Your *pelvis* must *tilt upwards*.

The quality of your *dynamic balance* will depend upon the quality of these six points.

1. Your eyes are vital for anticipating changes in terrain and if your eyeline is horizontal your *perception* will be as accurate as it can be and your inner ear balance mechanisms will function most effectively.
2. The most appropriate and normal response of your body to cope with speed is to flex and lower. As you learn to cope with speed, progressively straighten up and then you will have more 'flex in reserve' to cope with higher speeds.

A promising young Bulgarian, Borislav Kiriakov, copes well with high speeds in giant slalom

Despite aggressive skiing with rapid changes in body shape, Bojan Križaj keeps his eyeline horizontal

63

Boris Strel, bronze medallist in the 1982 World Championships, shows a powerful flexing of his outer ankle. His racing boots, although 'stiff', flex easily because of his weight and his strength

Nic Fellows, using the 'foot forward' technique in a slalom in Italy, maintains excellent dynamic balance—feeling that he is standing above the centre of his feet when they are pressing down into the snow

3. Flexion of the legs at the *ankles* is most important, both to bring your body mass forwards and, most of all, to stabilise the many bones forming the arch of your foot.

In order to apply pressure effectively through the balls of your feet, your boots must allow easy flexion of your ankles.

Note when you are out jogging, for example, your (running) shoes are worn down on this part of the sole and how, when you run in a circle, your ankle flexes and you push off and land on the ball of the foot.

In skiing such propulsive movements are quite small in comparison to running, as gravity supplies the motive power and so the heel can assume its role of supporting the body's weight. Your *'support, but ready for action'* posture, therefore, will use the *whole length* of your feet and developing awareness will permit efficient use of the feet in *dynamic balance*.

4. Your centre of mass, located in the centre of your body an inch or so below the navel (when upright), will not be above your feet when you are moving, but the resultant of all the forces acting upon you must still pass through your feet (see paragraph 3 above) and, therefore, you will *feel* that you are standing or pressing *against* your feet rather than on them.

The next two aspects of *dynamic balance* posture are the least emphasised, if at all, by most ski schools and yet they can have a very dramatic effect on your skiing.

To help you remember them I have given them 'catch phrase' names—the 'hoop' and the 'pelvic tilt'.

It is possible for an experienced coach to see virtually all he needs to know about your balance by looking at your hoop and your pelvic tilt.

5. _The hoop_ The shape of your arms and hands will be related to the muscle tensions in your shoulders and in your lower back.

Dynamic balance will be facilitated by having the arms held away from the body, relatively straight and hanging in a loose but controlled manner from the shoulders. The shoulder blades should be 'open', not pulled together on your back, and your lower back should be almost straight, not hollowed.

The ski stick grip—the centre of your fist—should be in line with the main, lower bone (the _ulna_) of your forearm. This ensures that the muscles on each side of all your joints are in appropriate tension or 'tone' and that when you plant your ski stick the force will be transmitted through the most stable form of joint.

To help you visualise (and feel) the best shape for your arms, imagine a bird's eye view of a large hoop.

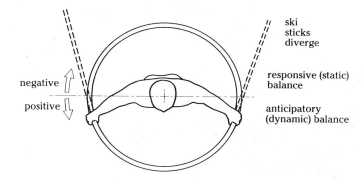

ski sticks diverge

responsive (static) balance

anticipatory (dynamic) balance

negative

positive

The hoop

Stand at the centre of the hoop and take hold of its rim, _forward of its diameter_.

On this part, the positive side of the hoop, your balance will be enhanced, your body and arms will be 'closed' in the front and your _ski sticks will be diverging_.

Ingemar Stenmark, World and Olympic Champion, and many times World Cup winner. After small losses in balance he returns to good posture and regains his 'hoop' more quickly than most other racers

A potential loss of balance during a sharp turn is prevented by a quick return to his 'hoop' by Bojan Križaj

The image on the left shows a severe downward pelvic tilt. The middle image shows the pelvis tilted upwards to its full extent. The image on the right shows the most appropriate amount of pelvic tilt for skiing

Good dynamic balance cannot be achieved if the upper body is too upright, the lower back hollow, or the elbow(s) pulled backwards

As you bend and straighten whilst skiing, try to keep hold of your hoop—loosely. Move it forwards as you bend down and back again as you straighten, but on no account allow yourself to hold the hoop behind its diameter.

When you are skiing relatively slowly you will use quite a small hoop, but as your speed increases you will find you will benefit from using a larger diameter hoop.

Try to keep it in its 'original' shape, and notice how, under stress, you distort it, squeeze it and tilt it. At your first feelings of stress or losing control—*check your hoop!*

6. ***The pelvic tilt*** (the seat tucked under) In Chapter Three I wrote of the importance of good posture and gave you some exercises to improve your posture.

If you have been doing those exercises you will be able to improve your skiing dramatically by tilting your pelvis when you are skiing.

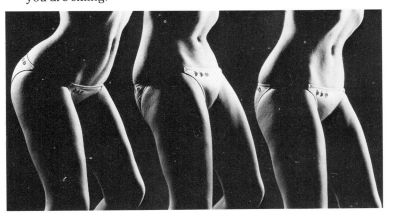

Movements of the hips, backs and legs necessary for good dynamic balance will all be inhibited if your pelvis is tilted downwards.

The first signs that will show you if *you* need to tilt your pelvis upwards are easily recognised:

○ your balance is not as good as it could be
○ your arms may be bent and your elbows pulled backwards
○ your lower (lumbar) spine will be very curved
○ your legs may be stiff and you may be unable to 'get off your heels'
○ when you angulate in your turns, your hip will move out sideways and you will find it difficult to edge effectively.

These symptoms are often responses to fear or high anxiety, and may show up at moments of stress. If they have already become habitual, it may be through earlier learning whilst either tired or defensive.

Check these symptoms when you are skiing and if you are aware of any of them, work on the basic posture exercises and, before you set off on every run, check that you have tilted your pelvis upwards slightly—'tuck your seat in before you go'!

So far, I have spoken of achieving *dynamic balance* and you may have inferred from this that a stillness, a fixed position, is required. Nothing could be further from the truth.

No one can maintain balance without moving, however small and subtle the movements might be.

Try this exercise now—stand on one foot and try to keep very still. Do you feel the small movements that occur in your legs and arms and, most of all, inside your foot?

From now on think not of balance but of the process of *balancing*.

Dynamic balancing is best sought with a calm mind and body. Unfamiliar movements and sensations will often raise your anxiety 'over the top of your curve' and will interfere with your balancing. *When your balance is threatened all the other three fundamentals take second place.* To reduce this possibility, do some exercises to test your balancing to its limits.

The inside edge of your foot is best suited for controlling your movements but, if you can use the outside edge of your feet as well, you will be that much more versatile.

1. Firstly, on easy terrain, try lifting your lower foot in a traverse, then later lift your lower ski during a diagonal skid.
2. When you have managed that, try lifting your outside ski off the snow, when you are turning.
3. Another good exercise is to ski with the clips of your boots undone—you will immediately become aware of how much you normally rely on your stiff, high boots. With the clips undone you won't be able to stand on your heels or toes, you will be forced to stand on your whole foot and bend your ankle too in order to stabilise your foot.

In these and all other skiing movements when your balancing is being tested, remember to keep calm, lower your shoulder blades (go on, try that now) and take hold of your 'hoop'.

Sarah Lewis checks her pelvic tilt and demonstrates excellent dynamic balance. Her right arm is bending as she prepares to plant her ski stick

Robbie Hourmont, outstanding winner of the British Children's Championships, 1982, with an excellent 'hoop', posture and versatile balance

Dave Stanley enjoying the summer snow in Val Senales

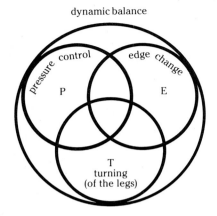

dynamic balance

pressure control

edge change

P

E

T
turning
(of the legs)

One final tip—always try to keep your head over your support foot.

It is important at this point to remember that *every turning technique* contains the four fundamentals.

Consider the diagram as three circles within a bubble—the bubble of *dynamic balance*. If it bursts, the circles fall apart and you find yourself lying in the snow.

Each circle overlaps the other, each fundamental controlling factor is essential to achieve any turning technique and each affects the others. Each factor must be balanced in harmony with the others. If any one is performed out of harmony, then good dynamic balance is forfeited.

The bubble of *dynamic balance* may burst from the outside—by failure to adapt to outside forces from the terrain—or from the inside, by disproportionate emphasis on one or other of the factors—*leg turning, edge control or pressure control*.

Remember that all three are used in every turning technique, in different sequences and varying degrees, according to your objectives.

Turning

Turning in this diagram means simply altering the direction in which the ski is pointing. Skis are held onto the boots by bindings and effective and efficiently controlled turning of a ski is achieved simply by rotating your leg. It is possible to turn your skis by other means, for example throwing your upper body around, but this is a most inefficient way of *controlling* the direction in which a ski points.

The 'rear' image shows Sarah with her legs aligned in her forward plane. They then *turn* (rotate) to her right, independently, and incline as they edge. Note the medial rotation of her left leg relative to her pelvis

Skilful skiing utilises a relatively inactive upper body with active *rotation* of *both legs*, independently of each other.

In all our normal athletic activities we use our legs separately and independently. To be a skilful skier you must always keep both legs working independently of each other, even if, at times, it looks as if other experts work them as one. Do not confuse 'having the legs close together' with lack of independent leg action.

Each leg turns separately in its own hip socket and must always be free to do so.

Flexion and extension

It is very difficult to rotate your leg (and so turn your ski) with your legs straight. Try stubbing a cigarette out with your foot, and notice that it is easier with your leg bent. Next time you are using a screwdriver, notice that you can bring more power to the turning screw by bending or straightening your arm as you drive. So it is with skiing. You will be able to turn your legs more easily if you flex or extend slightly *while* turning.

This flexing and extending facilitates turning of the legs, because of the way the leg muscles are attached and the way they contract to produce power. It should not be confused with unweighting, which depends upon more rapid movements.

Axis of rotation

One end of the axis around which your leg rotates should always be in your hip socket, the head of your femur—your thigh bone—but the axis may pass through any part of your foot (or, indeed, outside your foot in certain cases).

Sarah's right leg, initially turned outwards (relative to her pelvis and the front plane of her torso) rotates medially as it extends to meet the snow, and then rotates even more as it flexes again

The axis of rotation arises in the hip socket and passes through the centre of Sarah's foot in this turn. Note the excellent pelvic tilt and coordinated yet independent leg action

At a given speed, a carving ski will follow a predetermined arc. Note that Sarah's outer leg does not rotate at all (relative to her pelvis and torso) during this long radius turn. This illustrates the need to *aim* accurately along a curved line, if the need to correct the carving line by small rotations of the leg is to be avoided

Where the axis is, or where the pivot point in the foot is, will usually depend on which part of the foot is carrying your 'weight'.

It will be valuable to practise turning by pivoting on both toes and heels. Sometimes you will turn an unweighted ski and in this case pivoting around the centre of your foot is usually most efficient.

At this time, it will be worth considering the shape and flex of the ski again. It is often said that a 'weighted ski' on its edge will 'turn' on its own—it will carve—and, therefore, it could be argued that, in some forms of racing and advanced skiing, *it is the carving ski which turns the leg and not the leg which turns the ski.* This is sometimes true for some turns with a large radius. However, the radius of such turns cannot be effectively controlled, being dependent upon the shape of the ski only, and so small adjustments to a carving turn will need to be made by very small rotational movements of the leg. It is always a question of degree.

The mechanical efficiency of your leg turning will be affected by the shape of your upper body. This will be considered further in Chapter Eleven.

Edging

This is the lateral tilting of your skis and is important in two respects.

1. It is the action which moves the ski *into* the snow.
2. It is the action which controls *the resistance* that the snow will then offer to the skis.

I have heard many skiers talking of 'setting an edge' or 'making

an edge set'. They think that their skis should be either fully edged or not edged. But one of the important differences between skilful and habitual skiers is that the skilful skier can 'edge' his or her skis very precisely and appropriately.

Try the following exercise while standing on flat ground and then again during long turns on a gentle slope.

Start with one ski flat on the snow, roll it over and 'edge' it severely. Feel the flat ski as having a 'value' of 0 and the severely edged ski having a value of 4. Alter the amount of edge progressively from 4 to 0 and then again from 0 to 4 giving intermediate stages, values 1, 2 and 3. Be aware of what 'value

Dennis Edwards, after changing pressure from his left to his right ski, extends and moves across his skis, and thus changes his edge with this inward inclination of his legs

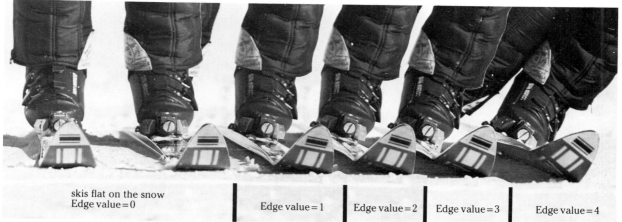

skis flat on the snow
Edge value = 0   Edge value = 1   Edge value = 2   Edge value = 3   Edge value = 4

71

edge' you are applying at different parts of the turns and, very soon, your ability to control your edges precisely and efficiently will improve dramatically.

So far I have not told you how to edge. This will normally be done during turning, within a movement and body shape known as *angulation*, but because this involves the four fundamentals, I will consider angulation in Chapter Ten.

Many ski instructors use catch phrases when they are teaching and, if you are not careful, you may sometimes miss the important parts of the movement and instead focus on the catch phrase. Just such a catch phrase is: *to edge, 'push your knees in'*.

It is true that your knee moves sideways when your lower leg is tilted to edge a ski, but to concentrate on this *only* will produce many inefficiencies in your skiing. If *all* you do to edge is push your knee sideways then you will be twisting your leg and putting yourself in a potentially dangerous shape. Your hip will still be above your foot and, should the ski slow down or stop *before* the binding can release, you will twist your leg, leading with your hip. In the same situation, but where the ski slows down only slightly, then the outward swing of your hip will cause an unwanted skid which you will not be able to control however much you try to 'push your knees into the hill'.

Because women's femurs angle inwards towards the knees, more hip angulation is necessary (than for men) if the hip is not to move outwards when the leg is rotated in order to steer the ski. In order to edge and steer her left ski efficiently, this lady skier should have her head and upper body further out over her ski, thus angulating more at her hips

What should you do instead? The answer is, fortunately, quite simple. Although the knee is at the top of your lower leg and thus moves in when you edge, it is also at the lower end of your thigh. You should become aware, then, of moving your *thigh in* to edge. To keep in balance, you will need a certain amount of looseness in your hips and back, but using your *knees and thighs* to edge will give you effective safe control over your skis. Moving the *thigh* in separates edging from turning, which also occurs when you 'push your knee in' only.

Wide stance

All modern ski schools now teach beginners to ski with their skis and feet apart. It is believed that this is because it is easier to balance, because the beginner has a wider base. This is true, but it is only part of the reason.

One of the disadvantages of having the skis close together is that any attempt to 'edge' the outer ski of a turn, or the lower ski in a traverse, often results in the inner or upper ski being put onto its outside edge. We have seen in the section on dynamic balance that the foot uses its inside edge for effective and efficient control, and thus the use of the *wide stance*—skiing with the feet slightly apart—enables learners of all levels of ability to use and develop awareness of the *inside edge* of the foot, without having to move either foot to do so. The importance of the 'wide stance' should not be underestimated—just watch the world's best racers, to see how they keep effective edge control and independent leg action. It also provides for effective 'leg lean in' with minimal movement.

Nic Fellows, with accurate attack (note the shapes of his two skis), moves his whole thigh inwards to edge, *as* he turns his outer leg

This young racer suffers from wrong early learning when he held his feet too close together, thus preventing effective use of the outer ski. Notice how his outer ski is *not* in reverse camber, because the pressure is spread over both skis

One of the top slalom skiers in the world, Bojan Križaj, evidences very active, independent leg action during his slalom training

Bengt Fjallberg, rising Swedish star and bronze medallist in the 1982 World Championships. His skis turn only after (a) a transfer of pressures to his new outer ski—first and second images, (b) a change of edges—third image—PET

Pressure control

This means simply adjusting the pressure exerted on one or both skis and/or from one part of the skis to another part.

I have considered both turning the skis (to alter the direction in which they point) and edging the skis (to control the potential snow resistance) but neither of these movements can have any effect on *the direction in which you travel* unless the skis are *in* the snow and under *pressure*.

It is the *pressure* between the snow and the skis which is essential to steering the skis, but this can only be controlled by body movements above the skis.

The essential source of *pressure* is your mass. The effect of gravity on your mass is to give you weight and the diagram shows how your weight will be transmitted by your skis and achieve a *distribution of pressure* between skis and snow.

The pressure distribution along the length of a ski varies according to the make and the model. In general, compared with sport models, slalom skis exert higher pressure under the shovel, and giant slalom skis exert higher pressure under the foot and lower pressure under the shovel.

The example shown in the diagram, with a skier weighing 143 lb, yielded the following pressure measurements at points A, B and C. Different models from one manufacturer were used.

		A	B	C
competition skis	slalom	13	82	8
	giant slalom	7	94	4
recreation skis	sport	10	85	7

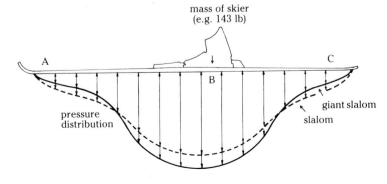

To ensure that *all* his weight is carried only on one ski, in order to achieve maximum reverse camber and accuracy in pressure control, Paul Frommelt of Liechtenstein lifts his inside ski *before* he changes edge and begins to turn

Pressure distribution is a function of both the camber and the flex pattern of your skis and it is for this reason that pairs of skis, even of the same model, may behave differently if either their flex pattern or camber is different. It is often the precision with which these two factors are matched from one ski to another within a single pair (many makes of skis are made in single moulds, rather than in pairs) that determines the 'quality' and, thus, the price of a *pair* of skis.

At first glance, it might appear that you cannot do very much (during a ski run) to change your weight, so how can you affect the pressure distribution at your skis? In fact there are several ways in which this can be done, all of which require co-ordinated movements of your muscles.

Weight

Simply by standing above or against one ski rather than both you will change the pressure at your skis. As this can vary from *all on one* to *all on both*, spreading the load between two skis can be very difficult to control accurately, especially during a turn, where pressure control is more important than during a straight run.

Ingemar Stenmark is reported once to have said to his equipment service man: 'You needn't file those' (the outside edges of his skis), 'I don't ski on my outside edges anyway.'

Of course, he does, in stepping and skating, but Stenmark, as does every good skier, controls the pressure against his working (steering) ski very accurately by keeping his weight completely off the inner ski when he is turning. Every time the inner ski 'pads' down, the load is spread between both skis and so the pressure distribution on the outer ski will change.

The effects of carrying body weight (or momentum when moving) on one ski only, or of sharing it between two skis equally, can be seen in the shape of the skis, correspondingly deformed

Martin Bell, a truly excellent young Scottish skier, extends rapidly 'downhill' across his skis, and thus becomes unweighted at his maximum extension

With a firm stick plant, this Swedish skier, Michael Berg, unweights his skis, and maintains superb dynamic balance

The ski stick is planted immediately prior to an edge change, and can be used, with good posture through a strong upper body, to support you momentarily while you begin to turn. Do not become too reliant on your stick for support, though; use it mainly as an aid to timing your movements

At low speeds and during skidded turns this facility will enable you to balance and control your turns easily but, as you improve your balance, strength and courage and want to carve your turns occasionally, then changes in the pressure distribution from one ski to another during the turn are undesirable.

Unweighting

This is the standard skiing term for actively removing the pressure between skis and snow. The same movements which can be used to 'unweight' your skis can also be used simply to reduce the pressure and this often requires less effort and gives greater control.

There are, basically, four ways of unweighting.

Up-unweighting If you extend your legs rapidly, then at the end of the extension, the pressure between skis and snow will diminish completely. At the end of a gentle extension, a partial reduction in pressure is achieved. Your timing is important here, because the pressure is not reduced at all during the extension but only at the high point.

Down-unweighting If you flex your legs rapidly, during this action the pressure is reduced. For a complete removal of pressure your legs must bend more quickly than they would if they simply collapsed and allowed the body to fall under gravity. For this reason, down-unweighting is used to achieve subtle changes in pressure, and for greater control and precision in timing is often used in conjunction with a stick plant.

Stick planting A firm planting of your stick will cause a change in pressure between your skis and the snow. The effect is the same as

that achieved by 'padding' the inner ski down during a turn. If you share your weight between several points of support, the pressure at any one of them will be less than if it alone carried your weight.

Plant your stick, accurately and firmly, and for as long as you continue to press on it you will be reducing pressure at your skis. It is for this reason that skilful skiers time the planting of their stick at precisely the right moment—the moment when they want to change pressure at the skis, in order to stop turning one way and begin to point their skis in a new direction—the moment when they want to begin a new turn.

Terrain unweighting At the extreme end of this scale, skiing off the end of a cliff will cause a rapid and complete removal of pressure at your skis. Under more normal skiing conditions, movement over convex terrain will produce the same effect to a lesser degree. If you want to use this feature of the terrain you must, therefore, co-ordinate your movements with the terrain, through watching closely for the subtle changes in shadows and smoothness of snow surface in the terrain ahead.

As Sarah's skis move over this mogul, they become unweighted, and thus considerably easier to turn in the next fraction of a second

It is equally important to remember that, as your ski moves over convex terrain, it will undergo a reduction in pressure and this will be undesirable if you are in the middle of a turn. Your tip or tail may lose grip completely and, therefore, you must be in good dynamic (anticipatory) balance, or, if you are carving, or steering a partially carving ski, then you must extend the leg during this phase, in order to maintain the pressure against the ski.

Leverage

One further means of changing the pressure against your skis is by using your lower leg and ski boot as a lever. Tilt forwards and you will cause an increase in pressure at the front of the skis and likewise backwards.

77

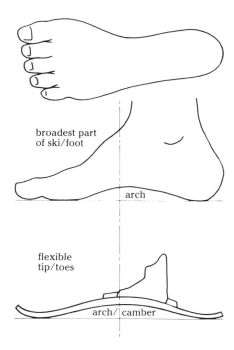

broadest part
of ski/foot

arch

flexible
tip/toes

arch/camber

The relationship between the shape of the ski and the
foot is clearly seen in this diagram in which the cross-
section of the ski has been somewhat exaggerated.
'You' are attached behind the centre of the length of
the ski/foot

In many ways the ski is very similar to, and certainly acts as an
extension of, your foot.
  ○ It is long and supports you.
  ○ It has an arch.
  ○ It is more flexible in the front than at the heel.
  ○ It is broader at the front than anywhere else.
  ○ You are attached to it nearer to the heel than to the toes.
  It is not surprising, therefore, that if you consider your ski to be
an extension of your foot and then use your foot normally, as you
would in most athletic activities, leverage of your ski boot will
magnify the increase in pressure on the shovel of your ski that will
occur when you press against the ball of your foot and its inside
edge.
  Forward leverage also permits you to use your lower leg and
boot to lever pressure at the front of the ski (in order to start a
turn, say) when you may, in fact, be standing along the whole
length of your foot—as is desirable for good dynamic balance.

Fiona Pulsford, after pressing her left ski into the
matting, remains balanced against the centre of her
ski; but by driving her shins forward, this leverage
through her boots causes the front of her ski to
deform and to lead the rest of it into a carved,
accurately steered turn

78

As Bojan Križaj finishes this turn, he extends his left leg to maintain effective steering pressure, and in so doing, his calf presses his boot shaft backwards and contributes to the reverse camber in the heel of his ski, *without* his mass moving backwards

Modern, high-backed ski boots also permit backward leverage. The specific advantage of these boots is not only that they keep you upright when you lean or lose balance backwards but, much more importantly, they will enable you to exert back leverage by moving your lower leg backwards, while at the same time your body remains in good posture and balance over the centre of your ski.

The four fundamentals of turning techniques
Dynamic balance is a function of the whole body and involves considerable attention initially to the arms and upper body. Once a good dynamic balance mode is achieved, however, the remaining three fundamentals are, essentially, functions of the skis which are achieved by sensitive, independent control of your legs.

Chapter nine

Learning How to Turn, Steer and Carve

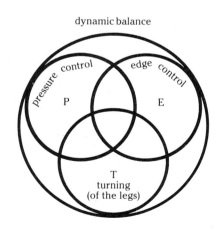

In the last chapter we saw how the four fundamental controlling factors can be considered separately, while recognising them as interdependent constituents of every turning technique.

There are several advantages of looking at turning on skis in this way.

Firstly, the complexity of all ski schools' turning techniques can be reduced, simplified to these four elements.

Secondly, most of your technical problems can be traced to weakness in one or other of these four elements.

Thirdly, all *four fundamentals* are subject to kinaesthetic awareness. You will be able to feel what you are doing and experience the consequences of your movements, rather than simply learning stylised body movements, or, even worse, stylised body shapes, in isolation from their consequences; and, fourthly, you will not be limited by your previous learning.

Many skiers claim that 'learning parallel turns has been inhibited by learning stemming or snow ploughs'. This will not happen to you if, while you appear to be snow ploughing, what you are actually doing is investigating one or more of the 'four fundamentals'.

Proficiency in the 'fundamentals' will increase your ability to ask your body (and skis) to do whatever you wish it (or them) to do. This is the essence of skilful skiing—small variations on any technique theme will be accomplished with ease and, most important of all, you will be able to solve many more skiing problems and learn and develop many more advanced turning techniques simply by changing the *emphasis* and the *sequence* of the last three fundamentals.

Balancing is required continuously, so from now on you need only consider three fundamental factors (in the inner circles). I have said in the previous chapter that *skiing turns* are characterised by their differences. I also said that all turning techniques have the *fundamentals* in common.

How then do the differences in turning techniques arise?

The differences arise from the sequence of application of the three fundamentals, specifically in respect of which of the three fundamentals occurs first, and the amount of emphasis on each 'fundamental'.

For example, *stem christies* and *short swings* both begin with a *turning* of the leg(s) followed by an *edge* change (usually occurring *before* the initial turning of the leg is complete) followed by an increase in *pressure* on the outer ski of the coming turn.

In simple terms then, stem christies and short swings are both:

T+E+P=TEP sequences.

The difference between them arises from the amount of leg turning and the rate of same, plus the speed of pressure change and its intensity—smooth and gentle in stem christies and sharp and heavy in short swings.

It is slightly complicated, of course, by the fact that these fundamentals apply to *two* legs, which may work one at a time, as in stem christies, or both together (independently but simultaneously) as in short swings.

Short swings have, in addition, strong rhythm.

In simple terms again, then:

Stem christies = TEP: outer leg initiated
(*outer* refers to the coming turn)

Short swings = TEP: both legs initiated

It is worth noting that if you can recognise this analysis when you practise, and add a strong rhythm to your stem christies, you will be doing a form of short swing that many junior racers practise.

To help you further appreciate the *sequence* used in turning techniques, do the following investigations next time you go to the ski slopes.

What is the sequence (e.g. TEP) of

1. Snow plough turning, done from a schuss?
2. Stem turn?
3. Basic swings in an elementary form?
4. Basic swings in a developed form, when they are nearly parallel?
5. A plough swing, from a plough in the fall line?

And with which leg (outer leg, inner leg or both legs simultaneously) do you initiate the sequence of the turn about to be made?

There you have five exercises with five sequences to be identified and thought given to which leg initiates the sequence in each case.

I am not going to give you the answers, as you should discover them for yourself, but if you believe you can work them out, then do see if you can 'feel' the answers in action when next you ski.

In Chapter Eleven you will see how turning your skis across the direction of your momentum will cause you to skid.

This information, combined with an awareness of the 'fundamentals', can improve your skiing very rapidly.

An example: Many skiers, intermediates as well as beginners, have difficulty in making a well-balanced, controlled skid. Indeed, although many 'good' skiers would argue that they are 'advanced' because they can carve a turn (i.e. not skid), it is my observation that they are 'advanced' skiers only when they are able to skid, easily and in efficient control, because they have good control of their 'fundamentals'.

TEP: While her skis are unweighted, Sarah *turns* her legs and thus puts her skis at an angle to her momentum; after changing the *edges*, the skis then come under *pressure* as they meet the snow again. Thus TEP produces *skidding*

What do all skidded turns have in common?

We have seen that the skis must turn across momentum, and this is certainly easy to do if the skis have little or no snow resistance when they are turned. Therefore, TEP—*turning* the ski(s) just before or while changing the *edge* before applying *pressure* to it—will cause the ski(s) to skid.

Skidding is very valuable, not only because it enables you to control your speed easily and quickly but because it is a means by which you can practise leg turning.

Young children

It is very important that young children be encouraged to skid a great deal.

This is especially true if they are either in, or hoping to take up, training for racing. Why should this be, when good racing means learning to carve?

Firstly, because it will give them an excellent 'feel' for the 'fundamentals'.

Secondly, because it will enable them to learn to turn their legs (rather than their hips and legs) and develop good posture, dynamic balance and angulation.

Thirdly, it will give them quick stopping ability, and this will raise their confidence. After all, you are prepared to drive your car fast only if you know your brakes are working.

Fourthly, and this is perhaps the most important reason, it will enable them to learn how to turn their young legs (muscles, joints and ligaments) under conditions of *low resistance*. This is how all physical training should be for young children.

As their ability increases they can increase, *slowly*, the 'load' in training, by increasing the speed and thus the centrifugal effect of their weight, and by increasing the amount of edge they apply during their turns.

This will ensure that as they improve their skiing, their legs can increase in strength in turning movements (which put great stress on their legs) in a manner appropriate to their physical growth.

It is interesting to note that there has been an increase in knee damage in young skiers recently. This is not so much because of injury but for many reasons, some of which are still being studied. One reason, certainly, is the tendency to use stiffer boots and longer skis than they would have done ten or fifteen years ago, to go faster. This equipment makes it easier to carve rather than skid and, together with 'racing' in moguls or ruts (which give a carving action), this modern fashion for everyone to learn to carve is having an injurious effect on young children.

This does not mean that young children should not carve, only that they should learn to skid, a great deal and often, first.

They should also use short skis and, most important of all, soft, forward-flexing ski boots.

If you are not a young child, or even if you are, and you have learned to 'skid a lot' you will be quite good by now at 'TEP-ing'!

Sasha Orr, a young English skier with considerable promise. She shows here good dynamic balance and technique, but hints of tension can be seen in the angle of her head and the slight cocking of her right wrist

Perhaps you have been skiing for many years and are very good at 'TEP-ing' but cannot quite cut out the little stem when you try to ski parallel. You can, but you still have to hop a little? I have a lot of sympathy for you. I was in that position for a long time and my ski instructors always told me that everything was OK and that all I had to do was

○ reduce the stem,
○ reduce the hop,
○ reduce the skid,

and I would soon be able to ski like them.
Well, it wasn't true then and it isn't true now!

○ A reduced stem is still a stem,
○ a reduced hop is still a hop, and
○ a reduced skid is still a skid.

The answer is, if you don't want to stem, hop or skid, *don't!* Do something else instead.

Easier said than done, you might say. Well, yes, but only if you are an habitual stemmer, hopper or skidder.

If you have learned how to stem or skid (I missed out hopping because that is only a quick 'two-legged' stem) by implementing the TEP sequence, and you have developed your awareness of these 'fundamentals', then I assure you that you will be able to do refined parallels with ease.

All you have to do to ski as you want to ski, to make smooth, refined parallel turns with minimal skid, is simply to *change the sequence!*

Momentum causes you to skid if your skis are turned across it

Despite an excessive step, with too high an arm, Sarah *presses* her outer ski into the mat; and then, with very good posture regained, she moves knee and thigh inwards and changes *edge* as she begins and then continues to *turn* her legs. PET for effectively and efficiently steered turns

The skidding caused by Sarah 'TEP-ing' was exaggerated in this case by the very powerful change in pressure which occurred when she landed suddenly on a turning ski

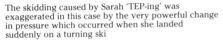

(TEP) but only if they are relatively unweighted at the time.

To initiate your new, refined, turn, all you have to do is change from TEP to PET.

As you *finish* one turn, your outer ski will be under pressure if you're in good dynamic balance. At this point, press your other foot (and hence ski) down into the snow and then as this ski now comes under *pressure*, smoothly change the *edge* (from outer to inner) and as you do so, begin to *turn* your leg (foot and ski) into the new turn.

You are now steering a weighted ski and—as in a car that is gripping the road—the likely amount of skid will be low, depending upon the state of the tread and the water or ice on the road.

As you are skiing on a very slippy and not very strong 'road' you are still likely to skid a little bit but if you PET sensitively you will feel a strong steering effect which you can turn into a *carving* effect with more practice and yet more sensitivity.

Powerful changes of *pressure* on the skis are likely to make the skis skid, especially if the change follows the *turning* of the ski, but a refined steering of your skis will be achieved as you become aware of, and can separately control, the three fundamentals of *pressure, edge* and *turning*, with an appropriate and sensitive *balance* between them.

Earlier, I showed you that stem christies are initiated with a movement of the *outer leg* of the coming turn. In order to reduce the stem to zero, to remove it completely, you will need to PET. You can achieve this most easily by shifting your attention from the outer ski of the coming turn (the one you would stem) to the *inner leg* of the coming turn.

Refined parallel turns are very difficult indeed to learn one at a time; it is best by far to develop refined turns while you are linking your basic turns with reasonable *momentum*. This will help you flow from one turn into the next and aid your *dynamic balance*.

As you are completing one turn, the outer ski of that turn will be under *pressure*. Put all your attention on that leg. It must not be fully bent. This leg—your 'outer' leg—is about to become the *inner leg* of the *next turn*.

Your skis are parallel now and you don't want to stem, so stop thinking about stemming and direct your attention back to your 'outer' leg. The ski is gripping, the snow pushing your ski along its curving path. Your leg is resisting the centrifugal effect of your *momentum*.

Your leg is wanting to bend a little more!

Now: let it—help it.

Bend your leg—the *inner leg* of the coming turn—remove your ski just off the snow.

This will have the effect of letting your momentum flow across your skis and help the new turn to start; it will also cause your other ski to become 'weighted'.

Austria's top young slalom racer Christian Orlansky begins his turns by lifting or 'removing' his outer support ski, which then allows his momentum to flow across his skis, and permits the new turn to start

As Dennis 'removes' his left ski, he extends his right leg in order to intensify the pressure against his right, and now steering, outer ski

You have changed the *pressure* to the new *outer* ski and now all you have to do is roll your thighs across to change the *edges* and then *turn* your skis in the snow and steer them around a smooth arc.

You can aid the pressure change, as soon as you have bent the *inner leg* of the coming turn, by extending the *outer leg* of the new turn. This will intensify the *pressure* change and put the ski in reverse camber if you change *edge* and begin to *turn* whilst still extending. Once the steering is under way, sink down into a comfortable, angulated 'middle' position and prepare for your next turn.

You will soon find that scissors turns and skating turns will be easy to learn now, now that you have mastered PET-ing as well as TEP-ing.

Before I finish this chapter, let me remind you to investigate the sequence of the fundamentals in the exercises I set you earlier. While you are doing that, see if you can recognise the sequence in every type of turn you can already do; then see if you can make up any 'new' turns by carefully going through different sequences.

To finish, I will leave you with another catch phrase to help you develop your refined, skilful skiing.

As a beginner you learned to ski by *'addition'*—*add* weight to your outer ski, *add* more edge to your turning ski, etc.

In order to flow more easily and make smooth, round, steered and carving turns, ski now by *'subtraction'*.

When you are moving well down the hillside simply *subtract* or *remove* the ski that is stopping you from turning into the direction that you now want to go in.

Think about it—then feel it in action.

Chapter ten

I have reserved a chapter for this concept because, although essentially simple and meaning little more than 'bending', it has acquired almost mystical significance to some skiers who, in attempts to demonstrate their use of this jargon 'in' word, somehow manage to achieve distorted postures and body shapes which interfere so badly with their skiing that their true potential will never be realised.

To be a skilful skier, you must be able to *angulate* both effectively and comfortably. Angulation should feel easy.

Before looking at 'how to do it', we shall consider what angulation is and why it is desirable.

'What is it?' is an easy question to answer, although small variations occur because of why it is done.

Angulation is essentially a bending *forwards* of the body at the *hips*, whilst simultaneously the *legs rotate* and incline inwards to enable pressure to be applied to the *inside edge* of the working (the outer or lower) foot and ski.

Angulation

Angulation: The features of efficient and effective angulation can be seen in Sarah's movements as she prepares to turn by tilting her pelvis slightly, whilst travelling forward. When her legs have turned relative to her momentum, they incline to balance the snow resistance force, and so she bends at her hips to permit her upper body to follow its momentum slightly. This forward flexion is clearly shown as her skis meet the extra resistance of the mogul in the foreground image

In his enthusiasm to attack the slalom course, Robert twists his upper body to avoid the slalom pole, and loses balance, 'falls' on to his inner ski, and loses time

Sarah, with excellent angulation, shows how the legs are turned with respect to her pelvis, which faces along a tangent to the arc of her turn. Her pelvis (approximate centre of mass) faces her instantaneous momentum, and her legs turn to steer her skis. Her upper body tends to follow its momentum while the skis create turning forces

The reasons why it is desirable to angulate are, firstly, because an efficiently angulated body will enable *leg rotation, pressure* control and *edge* control to be achieved most effectively; and, secondly, because it will be easier to maintain dynamic balance while controlling the other three 'fundamentals' during a change in direction of travel—a turn.

Angulation is essentially a dynamic activity and many skiers' problems arise from trying to learn it in a static situation. It is often interpreted as a bending sideways of the spine and this interpretation is sometimes reinforced with a twisting of the upper body, as often seen in slalom racers. The mistake here is to confuse angulation (effective steering and balance) with shoulder twisting (i.e. dodging slalom poles).

The twisting of the upper body away from the slalom pole is a totally separate movement from angulation and would not occur in the same skier at the same place if the slalom pole were not there.

Good angulation begins as a change in direction begins.

Good angulation is a movemement, not a position or body shape.

In any turning technique, a change in direction of travel begins when

  ○ an *edged* ski
  ○ under *pressure*
  ○ is *turned* at an angle to the original direction.

In order to *edge* and *turn* your ski effectively, your body should be flexed *slightly* at the hips. As your ski begins to turn, the pressure against it increases. (See Chapter Eleven.)

In order to remain in balance, therefore, you must have your leg inclined inwards to the turn (or out ahead and to the side of you if you look at it that way); otherwise you will 'trip' over, due to the centrifugal effect of your momentum. Your upper body will, however, tend to follow your momentum (*inertia*) and, therefore, by bending at your hips and allowing your upper body to flow with its momentum for a fraction of a second, your body will assume an angulated shape.

At slow speeds this movement is an active, forward movement of the upper body which brings the head over the turning/edging/pressing foot, but at higher speeds momentum takes the upper body forward and down, as the ski generates snow resistance.

Angulation is, therefore, a comfortable balancing response to turning forces at the feet, by a body which is made up of several different parts, each with its own momentum.

Angulation also has the mechanical advantage of enabling greater *edging* to be achieved than could be realised with a rigid body, by allowing your legs to incline inwards more than the line from foot to centre of mass.

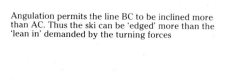

Angulation permits the line BC to be inclined more than AC. Thus the ski can be 'edged' more than the 'lean in' demanded by the turning forces

Hip and knee angulation

Keeping in good dynamic balance under continually varying terrain—ice, soft snow, bumps and hollows—while changing direction is a central problem in skiing and is a result of your *kinaesthetic perception* which I considered in Chapter Five.

Most of your feedback sensory information will come from your periphery—your feet, arms and head—but most of the controlling movements will be made with the muscles in the legs and lower abdomen and will be seen and felt as movements of the knees and hips.

All effective angulation will be *hip angulation*. This can be emphasised by actively moving your hips across your skis, at the end of one turn and the beginning of another. Thus, the edges will be changed and legs rotated more vigorously than if you came to 'neutral' between turns.

To achieve this movement you will need good kinaesthetic awareness. You will be aware of the different pathways through space that your feet and your hips are taking.

When you turn along an arc, your feet travel, as it were, around the bottom of a cone and your hips follow a smaller arc, higher up the cone. In very rapid turns such as in slalom or mogul skiing close to the fall line, your feet move along a series of linked arcs and your hips do likewise, except that their pathway is straighter.

When you finish one turn and then actively take your hips across

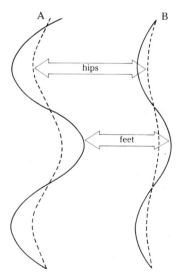

Typical routes in slalom gates: A. offset open; B. verticale closed. The dashed lines indicate the body momentum line, i.e. the pathway of the hips (centre of mass). The solid lines indicate the pathway of the feet (centre of skis)

Philip Harding uses a pronounced and very effective 'hip drop' in this turn, and thus changes his edges effectively and quickly. This technique enabled him to win in his age group in the 1982 British Championships

your skis, what you are in effect doing, therefore, is assisting them to follow as straight a line as possible down the hill. You are allowing the momentum of your upper body to be conserved whilst your legs and feet follow the skis in more rounded *S*-shaped pathways.

This feeling of 'dropping the hip' into the coming turn prepares you early for effective angulation which will control the turn when the skis are edged, turning and under pressure in the snow. When this pressure is great, due to high speeds or uneven terrain, good *hip angulation* is essential.

Refined control of your edging cannot, however, be achieved with *hip angulation* alone.

To travel on a turning ski requires delicate balance and so it must be possible to alter the degree of edging very quickly, without having to move any significant body mass which would require more time and strength. To do this *knee angulation* is used. Your knee should be moved forwards and to the inside of the turn. With this movement, you will achieve fine-tuning of edge and balance.

It is important to realise that knee angulation is used for *fine tuning*, because to attempt to use knee angulation *alone* to make turns is to invite difficulties and potential injury.

In order to move the knee medially (towards the centre of the turn) the thigh must be adducted (pulled towards the centre) and rotated. It is this rotation of the thigh which may produce the problems.

Excessive rotation of the thigh while attempting to keep the ski on an increasing edge will cause

○ the tail of the ski to break away if the snow cannot hold it,
○ or the hip to move outwards and so cause loss of hip angulation, or even negative angulation in extreme cases, with the consequent total loss of balance,
○ or excessive stress on the knee joint itself.

The knee is inherently a very weak joint. It is 'designed' only to bend in one plane (fore/aft relative to leg) and yet, with the appropriate muscle development, it can be very strong and, indeed, will carry more than your bodyweight with ease. As soon as the knee moves laterally or medially out of alignment with the hip and ankle, however, it immediately becomes unstable and relies entirely on ligaments and muscle strength to hold it in place.

For this reason, *knee angulation* should be used sensitively and correctly, that is, only to provide the fine tuning that is needed to make *hip angulation* most effective.

Safety note

You may observe that world-class racers appear to use extreme amounts of *knee angulation* in quick, successive *slalom* turns. Some indeed do, but it must be borne in mind that these are highly trained athletes who spend up to eleven months per year training and skiing, and their knees (and the muscles surrounding them) can cope with more stress than yours—or mine—can, travelling at similar speeds.

This young racer rotates her left thigh medially, but because of poor pelvic tilt (see her left arm and hollow back) her hip moves outwards and her skis skid

Anxiety and a poor pelvic tilt with loss of his 'hoop' mean that the more this racer tries to edge his right ski by turning his knee in, the more his hip will rotate outwards and cause his skis to skid

Chapter eleven

Mechanics

When you are learning, 'what it *feels* like' is much more valuable than 'what you *think* you are doing'. For this reason at least, mechanical explanations should be used in coaching situations sparingly and with discretion.

My aim in this chapter is to provide you with an additional tool for analysis, one through which you will be able to discriminate between superfluous style and fundamental techniques, and between effect and cause. An understanding of mechanical principles will enable you to understand better your observations of other skiers and will increase your confidence in the simple 'model' of skiing that I have presented to you.

The branch of mechanics which deals with motion resulting from the action of forces is called *dynamics*.

All motion in skiing, whether of the skier as a whole or of his distinct but integral parts, 'behaves' in accordance with long-established principles.

Motion is of two types, *linear* and *angular*. Linear motion is movement in a straight line and angular motion is rotational movement or movements along arcs.

Skiing movements are always a blend of linear and angular motion, except perhaps in a pure schuss, which could be considered to be purely linear.

It was as long ago as 1687 that Sir Isaac Newton stated the principles which govern the *dynamics* of skiing (and all other forms of motion as well). He embodied them in four now famous laws.

'Bodies' with mass attract each other

This law is obviously very important, and has become known as his 'Law of Gravity'.

For example, earth and apples, suns and planets, or more importantly, earth and skiers—all attract each other. We are very fortunate that Sir Isaac discovered this as it provides us with a very cheap power source. Ski lifts may be expensive to go up on but our source of motive power for skiing is *free*!

In order to control our bodies and influence the direction of our descents, however, his other three 'laws of motion' are of greater and more specific interest.

First law—'bodies' with mass have inertia

This law is particularly interesting because it explains, among other things, why we turn (alter our direction of travel).

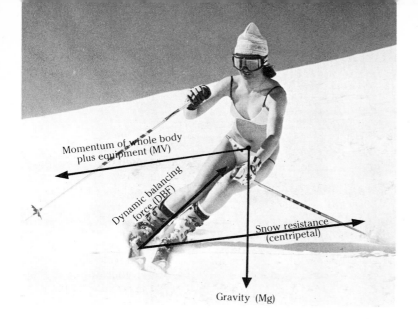

Momentum of whole body plus equipment (MV)

Dynamic balancing force (DBF)

Snow resistance (centripetal)

Gravity (Mg)

A body (a skier) will remain still, or *continue* to move with *uniform velocity* (i.e. same *speed* and direction) unless acted upon by an *external force*.

Thus, as a skier you need an external force to make you move: *gravity*, and then, once moving, if you wish to change your uniform motion, that is your speed and/or direction of travel, in other words, if you wish to *turn*, you must be acted upon by an . . .

. . . external force.

Where does this force come from and what is it called?

It comes from the snow and it is called

1. snow resistance

and

2. centripetal force—it forces your skis around a centre (due to the design of your skis).

An analogy will help to illustrate this. Consider the effect of a car (just) touching a wall.

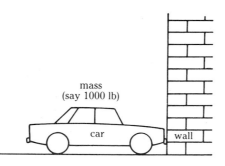

mass (say 1000 lb)

car

wall

Now imagine the car moving towards the wall.

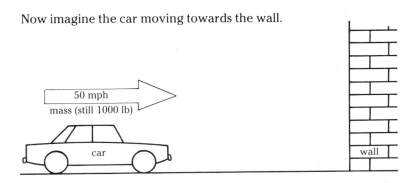

Now consider what happens when the car meets the wall.

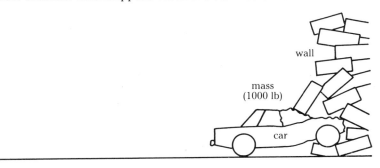

Newton's first law tells us that because of its inertia, the car tends to keep going (maintain its uniform velocity) and because of its inertia, the wall tends to remain stationary. The result is a *distortion* of the car and a *distortion* of the wall.

Now, for 'car' read 'skier and skis', and for 'wall' read 'snow'.

When the car with momentum (mass, speed and direction) hits the wall,	When a skier with momentum (mass, speed and direction) turns his skis at a slight angle to his direction of travel,
its *inertia* wants to keep it going straight on	his *inertia* wants to keep him going straight on
But the wall resists	But the snow resists
Result	*Result*
Distortion of the car	Distortion of skier (angulation) and distortion of skis (reverse camber)
and	and
Distortion of the wall	Distortion of the snow
'Look at the mess.'	'Look at your tracks.'

So Newton's law tells you why you turn—by creating *snow resistance* to your momentum which distorts you, your skis and the snow. Thus, by controlling these distortions—by leg turning, edge changing and pressure control—you can *direct* the resistance

of the snow in such a way that you control how quickly, how sharply, how roundly and smoothly, and how much you change your momentum.

Momentum is mass × velocity (speed and direction).

When you turn, you change your momentum. Your mass stays the same and so it is your velocity that changes. In this case both speed and direction will change.

Under normal circumstances, snow is much weaker than your skis and so will 'distort' or move much more easily.

Newton's law tells us that because of *inertia*, when you are skiing with momentum, your body (mass) will tend to maintain its *speed* and *direction* (uniform velocity) despite the *snow resistance*. Thus, if you turn your skis at a reasonable angle across your momentum then you will tend to keep going in the direction of your momentum, but with your skis moving sideways.

This is called *skidding*. Skidding is differentiated from side slipping.

Side slipping occurs when skis, sideways on to the fall line, are released from their edge grip. *Gravity* overcomes the *resistance* of the snow (acceleration occurs).

Skidding occurs whenever skis are turned at an angle to the (instantaneous) *direction of travel* and *momentum* overcomes the resistance of the snow.

When the moving body interacts with the snow, their momentum is shared and both are distorted. This sequence of Sarah Lewis is expanded in order to show the distortions (changing body shapes) clearly, but by so doing the momentum lines are curved more than in the actual skiing

As Karina turns her legs and skis across her momentum, indicated by the direction of her schuss, her inertia causes her to tend to continue in the same direction—sideways—skidding

95

Skidding occurs in almost every turn and is desirable in most forms for most skiers, as it reduces speed—uses a minimum of muscular energy to control the 'distortions' as a great deal of momentum is 'absorbed' by the snow—and permits fine tuning by leg rotation and edge control.

Carving occurs when the distortion of the skis is very precisely controlled, in such a way that the snow is only very slightly distorted. The snow and ski distort or deform in close harmony and the snow channels the deformed ski along the line of least resistance.

Ross Blythe, one of Scotland's best young skiers, member of the 1980 Olympic team. With excellent dynamic balance, he flies, lands and carves immediately. Note how he is holding his breath as he concentrates—regular breathing is very important, and Ross exhaled immediately after this photograph

Skidding on skis can be likened to turning your car at an angle to its momentum when the distortions in the tyres and road surface are too great to enable them to grip. Momentum 'overcomes' resistance and the car will skid sideways.

Carving on the other hand is rather like driving your car 'straight' around an appropriately banked 'wall of death' track. In this case, instead of the distortions being lateral in the tyres, they will be up the tyres and along the length (height) of the suspension legs.

Carving is desirable for some skiers who want to change direction of travel with minimum loss of speed.

Because the snow does not 'absorb' much of the skier's momentum and because excessive or inaccurate leg turning or edging will cause the snow to break away, carving can only be achieved by skiers with strong legs and very sensitive balance.

Carving is undesirable for skiers who have not yet learned to cope emotionally with speed but, for those who have, carving will give a sense of freedom and harmony with the terrain which must be used to control the speed potential which can now be realised from their skis.

Beginners and all other skiers must be able to make skidded turns, but when braking movements are not required, the exhilaration gained from feeling your skis work for you, using your choice of line to control your speed instead of resisting gravity all the time, are sources of intrinsic satisfaction in skiing.

The fear of falling gives way to the joy of flying.

Second law—the rate of change of momentum is proportional to the force causing it, and occurs in the direction of that force

Dynamic balance—a fundamental factor in all turning techniques —must, therefore, act in accordance with this law.

The meaning of the law can also be expressed in a simple formula.

Force	=	**Mass**	×	**Acceleration**
quantity and direction		quantity		rate of change of velocity (speed and direction)

A major significance of this law is that you must be aware that the forces acting upon you when you are skiing have direction, as well as 'amount'.

Good dynamic balance will only develop, therefore, when you become aware of the *direction* of your momentum.

On the face of it, this is obvious—your momentum has the direction that you are skiing in!

The only extra considerations arise because Newton's laws are really concerned with rigid bodies and skiers are far from rigid— well, good skiers are, at any rate!

This means that to become a skilful skier you must recognise

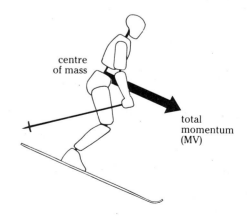

The skier's total momentum (MV), acting at his/her centre of mass, is the sum of the individual momenta of the parts of the body:
$$MV = m_1V + m_2V + m_3V + \text{ etc}$$
(see diagram overleaf)

centre of mass

total momentum (MV)

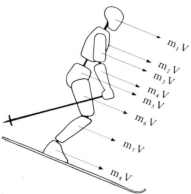

m_1V
m_2V
m_3V
m_4V
m_5V
m_6V
m_7V
m_8V

Turning in moguls. The peripheral parts of the body (head, arms, feet) follow different paths through space from that taken by the centre of mass. The centre of mass, having the most inertia, deviates least from a straight line

that all your 'bits', your legs, arms, body and head, all have mass and, therefore, they all have their own momentum.

When you develop awareness of your *total* or *central momentum* and, in addition, awareness of the momentum of your other moving parts, then you are said to have both *central* and *peripheral awareness*.

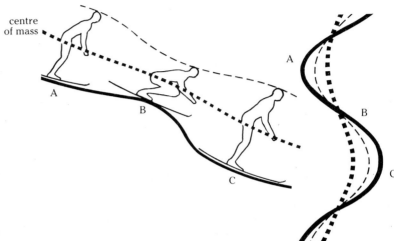

centre of mass

The other implication of the second law is that large changes of momentum are caused by large forces and, therefore, good dynamic balance will be achieved through *sensitive* control of the necessary *minimum* amount of movement in your different body parts, whilst recognising that your different 'bits' will often be moving in different directions from each other.

Understanding of this law will enable you to appreciate the two basic types of skiing that are commonly found on the ski slopes.

There is dynamic skiing, the basis of skilful skiing, but, sadly, there is also *static* skiing.

Static skiing is seen in people who are not aware of Newton's laws.

○Static skiing is also known as '*posing*':
○learning *positions* from books or instructors;
○or, worse still, *posing* as ski instructors (who pass it on);
○'How do I look?'

Third law—for every action (change in momentum) there is an equal and opposite reaction

The implications from this law for skiing are manifold indeed. It is often a matter of choice as to which 'movement' is the action and which is the reaction—in dynamics they exist simultaneously and are of equal importance. As we are concerned with motion originated and controlled by you, the skier, it is convenient to think of the skier as the originator of the force.

If you move your upper body there will be an equal and opposite reaction in your lower body (hips and legs). Conversely, whenever you move your legs to turn, there will be corresponding movement of the upper body. This will tend to upset your balance and may, therefore, require more compensating movements in the legs, etc.

It is clear, therefore, that movements initiated in the legs should be the positive ones, controlling your skiing, relating to the external forces which determine your movement down the slope; and that movements of the upper body should be kept to an absolute minimum, being essentially compensating movements to your leg actions, thus enabling good dynamic balance to be maintained.

This is especially true in racing and higher-speed recreational skiing, because the *distance* covered in the *time* that it takes to make unwanted movements can be significant.

Imagine you are skiing over a bump. If you do not use your peripheral awareness and you allow your arms to fly back, then you are likely to lose balance and, during that time, you lose the opportunity to control your skis effectively. It can take from half to over one second to pull your hands down again, from when you recognise that they have shot backwards.

By the time this young racer has pulled his arm back to a useful working position, he will have travelled approximately twelve feet—that is, he is out of control for a further six feet past the next gate in his race. He did in fact come out of the course two gates on

Distances along the snow that a skier will travel

		In 1 sec	In 0.1 sec
Recreational skiing	10–15 mph	14–22 ft	1½–2ft
Slalom racing	20+ mph	over 29 ft	over 3 ft
Giant slalom racing	50+ mph	over 73 ft	over 7½ ft

You can see from the table that all unnecessary movements should be reduced to a minimum. If your skiing posture is poor and you have to move your hand more than you need to to plant your ski stick at the start of a turn, if it takes two-tenths of a second more than it should do, in that time you will have travelled about four and a half feet, more than enough to upset your choice of line in a mogul field. Such a delay in three consecutive turns will mean that you will be over thirteen feet away from where you originally planned (or hoped) to be.

In reality, of course, you would probably take evasive action and turn without a stick plant, or hurry your next turns—in any event, all your movements must be controlled and co-ordinated, and in order to allow the legs to work quickly the upper body must be ready to balance and compensate.

An awareness of Newton's laws will enable you to evaluate your movements, but most of all you should develop an awareness of the results of your movements—be aware of the relationship between your skis and the snow.

Planting the ski stick

Before leaving behind mechanics, it will be valuable to look at principles governing specifically 'angular' or 'rotary' motion, for when skiing we 'turn' or rotate our legs; our whole bodies and our skis move along curved pathways. For this reason *angular momentum* is important.

Angular momentum is the amount of 'rotary motion' in a body and is a product of angular velocity and moment of inertia.

Angular velocity is measured in segments of a circle per unit of time, or more precisely, degrees or radians per second. For example, the angular velocity of the second hand on a clock is one complete revolution (360°) per minute or 6° per second.

When a skier performs short swings, the angular velocity of the (rotating) legs is approximately 60° per second.

Moment of inertia

We have seen from Newton's First Law that *inertia* (the reluctance to change momentum) is proportional to *mass*. In angular movement, however, the resistance offered to acceleration depends not only on the mass but also on its distribution about the axis of rotation.

This explains why it is easier to rotate your leg wearing short skis than when wearing longer skis.

In the skier's body, for example, the moment of inertia is greater if the arms are spread out and, as with ice skaters, bringing the arms in will enable the body to turn (rotate around a 'vertical' axis) more easily.

But skiers are not ice skaters, and unless you are a free-style/ballet skier (in which case the ice skater's moves apply) you will *not* want your upper body to turn when you are steering your skis.

The first part of this chapter has shown that movements of the legs should be the active generators of turning on skis, but when you try to rotate your legs, Newton's Third Law indicates that an equal and opposite (quantity of angular motion) effect will occur.

It is important that you ski with your legs acting independently, for all the reasons stated earlier, and because, in parallel skiing, part of the equal and opposite reaction to the rotation of one leg can be the rotation of the other leg (in the same direction but on the opposite side of your pelvis).

When you rotate your legs, with the skis in the snow, however, the forces involved are quite large and there will be a tendency for some of the equal and opposite reaction (to your leg rotation) to occur in your upper body.

You cannot prevent this from happening, although it is undesirable, as it means that poor balance and awkward posture may arise as your upper body twists in the opposite direction to your main working leg.

What you can do, however, is control it and reduce the angular velocity to a minimum.

How? By simply increasing the moment of inertia of your upper

One of the world's top slalom racers, Bulgaria's Peter (Pepi) Popangelov, increases the moment of inertia of his upper body, thus enabling him to rotate his unweighted legs very quickly for the next turn

body, relative to the axis of rotation. (The axis will pass through your foot, hip socket and on upwards.)

Spread your arms out and bend forward slightly at the hips (angulation). This will increase your moment of inertia (upper body) and thus increase the stability of your upper body, against which your legs can now turn easily, without any loss of balance being created.

When very quick turning action of the legs and skis is needed, you may very well choose to unweight as you begin to turn the skis. This will reduce the resistance to turning at the skis but the speed of movement required will demand an equally fast 'counter rotation' of your upper body. This is very undesirable as it will greatly upset your balance and disturb the flow of your movements downhill. Once again, you should increase your moment of inertia by spreading your arms and, ideally, increase the moment of inertia of your upper body massively, by adding to it a very large mass (just for the moment of starting the turn).

This can be achieved with powerful *isometric* contractions of your shoulder and arm muscles, so that when you *plant your stick* your upper body, for that moment, *includes* the mass of the earth (give or take the wobble at hand and stick point).

Thus, a powerful pole plant will increase the moment of inertia of your upper body and allow the active rotation of the legs to occur easily.

Planting the ski stick I have met many skiers who have been confused as to where they should plant their ski stick at the beginning of a turn. Some have been told to plant it 'close to the

With powerful but isometric use of his arm and shoulder muscles, Dennis Edwards momentarily attaches himself to the mass of the Earth with a firm pole plant, thus increasing the moment of inertia of his upper body massively, and can now make a powerful rotation of his legs to turn his skis

tip', others told 'half way between boot and ski tip', and many have been told to plant it in the triangle formed by boot, ski tip and an imaginary third corner 'down the hill from the ski tip'. Yet others have been told to plant it downhill of the boots. None of these directives is wrong, yet none is particularly useful, despite the fact that each instructor may have been quite correct at the time of giving the advice.

This is not because fashions in stick planting change, but because *where* you plant it will depend upon *how* you are turning.

Where you plant your ski stick should always be the same if it is to be of maximum effect, in timing, support in the upper body and triggering the new turn. It is *not*, however, planted in relation to your boots or your skis but in *relation to your momentum*.

You should plant your stick *just a little to the side* (towards the centre of the next turn) *of your momentum* with minimum movement of your arm.

On long turns, therefore, when your (total) momentum is travelling almost along your skis, you should plant your pole just downhill of your skis, but when you are making very tight, rounded turns, your skis will be almost at right angles to your momentum and so you will plant your stick still just off your momentum line, but now this will be out at the side and downhill of your feet.

To help you be aware of your momentum when you are turning, try to visualise what I call the 'conker' effect.

Imagine a bird's-eye view of a conker being whirled around on a string.

When the conker reaches point B (see diagram), it has angular momentum and *instantaneous linear momentum*—which is at right angles to the string and at a tangent to the arc, the path of the conker.

If the string were to be cut when the conker is at point B, then it would follow the direction of its instantaneous momentum. Angular momentum would cease and linear momentum would persist.

If you now imagine that this conker is you, then your 'momentum line' at any moment is at a tangent to the arc.

As we have seen earlier, however, only on long, fast carved turns will your centre of mass follow closely the path of your skis; in shorter, rounder turns, the momentum of your feet and skis will follow the *S*-shaped *arc*, but the momentum of your body, your centre of *mass*, will follow a much straighter pathway, nearer the fall line, and it is this pathway that is *your* momentum line. It is just to the side of *this* line that you plant your ski stick.

Mechanics and, specifically, dynamics is a study of the principles governing motion.

I hope that this chapter has indicated to you the importance of your momentum and some of the effects that it can have when you are skiing.

'What it feels like' is the important point to remember, and so if this chapter helps you to become more *aware* of your *central* and *peripheral momentum*, then it will have served its purpose.

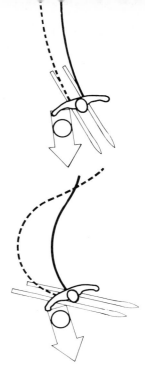

The ski stick is planted in a small area which is at a tangent to the path of your centre of mass (your momentum line). In long-radius turns (*above*) this area is adjacent to the path of your skis, but in short-radius turns (*below*) it is further out relative to the path of your skis

Below left: Alex Leaf shows a good 'hoop' in difficult snow conditions

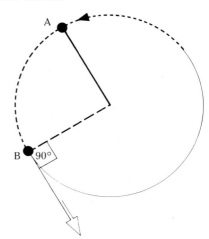

A conker being spun round on a string. At any point *A* along its arc, the conker has both angular momentum and instantaneous linear momentum. If the string snaps at *B*, the conker has linear momentum only, and flies off along the tangent to the arc

Chapter twelve

Skiing in Competition

Competition is not everyone's cup of tea. Indeed, the vast majority of holiday skiers find challenges enough on the varied runs that different ski resorts offer. Nevertheless, competitive skiing can offer positive rewards to the keen skier.

Competition against yourself, using external standards such as in the Junior and Adult Performance Award schemes, allows you to measure the technical quality of your skiing.

Participation in formal competition, which is often seen as 'man against man', is a means of setting yourself specific challenges, challenges which require effective application of your technical ability in a variety of situations and which also require considerable self-assessment and self-control.

Competitive skiing demands *skilful* skiing and can be seen as both a measure and a target for your developing skill.

Freestyle and racing

These are the two main forms of alpine ski competition and each is sub-divided into three sections. All require courage, technical ability, sound judgement and emotional control, but some are

Harti Weirather, downhill racing 1982 World Champion

One of the four wallcharts, available from the English Ski Council, which illustrate the Adult Performance Award Scheme

England's foremost freestyle coach and ex-British champion, Sarah Ferguson, illustrates a front crossover and a reverse reuel with good leg extension as she arches her back

intrinsically more dangerous than others and only four of these sections are easily accessible to skiers in Britain.

Aerial acrobatics in freestyle and *downhill* racing are both very specialised aspects of our sport, with an inherently high danger level. They must, therefore, be undertaken *only* with specialist facilities and expert coaching.

Freestyle

The two accessible disciplines in freestyle are *ballet* and *moguls*.

The whole structure of competitive freestyle skiing is as yet in its infancy and the rules are continually changing. I will, therefore, give an indication of what you may expect to do in these disciplines and give you a few pointers.

Ballet

The essential form of a ballet competition will consist of a graceful sequence of movements and manoeuvres, each linked and blending harmoniously one to another and with the terrain.

Judges will award marks which relate to the quality and control of your movements in personal space and to the way in which you use the available space on the slope. The difficulty of your manoeuvres is considered, as is your carriage, composition and choreography, in relation to your interpretation of your chosen music.

Ballet is a very 'creative' form of competitive skiing and every performance is what you make of it.

Irrespective of whether you ever participate in ballet competitions, learning the basic movements will help you to develop edge and steering control with considerable sensitivity.

Sarah, with a powerful take-off, spins, airborne about a good, straight, long axis. Spins and jumps are important ingredients of modern ballet sequences

You will find that knowing how to use all the parts of your skis—the outside as well as the inside edges, the heels as well as the tips, spinning on flat skis, skiing backwards as well as forwards—will improve your awareness and control of the *four fundamentals* and increase your confidence and turning techniques in a wider variety of situations than before.

Ballet skiing improves your skill.

Moguls

This is, in essence, a race against the clock, down a mogul field. You are free to choose your own line and you will be judged on your courage, control, quality of your turning techniques and also

Aerial acrobatics (page 105): Learning to somersault under strict control

the height, control and quality of any 'aerial leaps' that you may add. Your run will be accompanied by music and you must stop in a controlled manner in the finish area.

Mogul competitions are a test of fast, skilful 'free' skiing.

Learning to ski moguls well will improve your free skiing ability whether or not you ever enter a mogul skiing competition.

Moguls made easy Skiing down a mogul field is easy! It must be. After all the mogul field is only there in the first place because it is a popular route.

Moguls are not hayricks left by the farmers, or mounds built by giant moles but, simply, snowfields sculptured by countless descents of skiers.

Knowing how a mogul field is formed is part of the key to skiing it well. The other part is to remember the basic constituents of skilful skiing.

There are three approaches to skiing a mogul field and they depend more on your *emotions* and your *perceptions* than on your *techniques*.

If you *perceive* the mogul field to be a random array of icy bumps which get in your way, then your *emotions* will make it difficult for you to use your *technical* ability. If, on the other hand, you can *perceive* the structure and order in the moguls then you can decide on appropriate tactics to ski it skilfully.

Consider the skiers who made the moguls; up early after a fresh snowfall, they made longish, smooth turns down a field of virgin

Moguls made easy

A 'random array' of bumps, getting in the way!

107

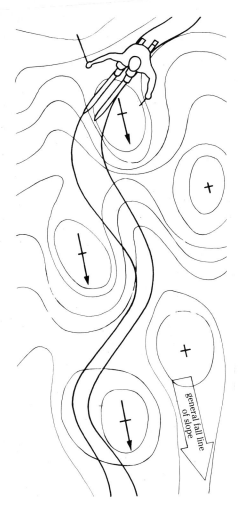

Contour diagram of moguls, their hollows and crests

general fall line of slope

snow. Others followed and the beaten pathways formed around mounds of snow pushed to one side. Later on, other skiers followed the early starters and, skiing more slowly, slid down the sides of the mounds, scraping them smooth.

The structure of the mogul field which you must look for is simply this:

A series of mounds with icy steep slopes on their downward sides, with softish snow approaches to their crests; try to recognise and pinpoint the exact summit of each mogul. More importantly, however, are the *pathways around and between* the moguls, in softish snow in the main, the pathways of the skiers who first made the moguls.

Once you *perceive* the mogul field in this way you will want to explore it and test your perception of it.

To begin with, traverse across the slope slowly and fold your legs over each mogul and stretch your legs and feet down into each hollow. When you feel comfortable, fold as you rise onto the crest and then, when tips and tails are 'free', swivel your skis around, slip down into the trough, recover your balance and then continue across the field. You are now going almost at right angles to the skiers who made the moguls but you are keeping your speed down and learning to recognise the structure of the mogul field very precisely.

Aim very precisely to cross the exact summit of every mogul in your path.

This is the first way to ski the moguls, hard work but it feels secure and is an excellent way, even for experts, to get to know the characteristics of a new slope.

A second way is simply to take up your courage, have faith in your ability to stay upright whilst you turn here and there, and simply 'go for it' down the fall line.

If you can do this, and you will know if you can when you look down a mogul field, then you don't need my help in this book.

Alan Hole demonstrates the 'bend and turn—stretch and turn' method for skiing over moguls at slow speeds

The third way is, in many ways, the most satisfying, as it is the easiest in terms of effort but demands great concentration and *selective attention* to your *pathway*.

This third way down a mogul field is simply to avoid the moguls altogether. Follow the hollows between the moguls and follow the pathways of the skiers who made them in the first place.

In order to balance your technique, emotions and perceptions, it is important to approach this method with serious care and attention.

1. *Stand* at the top of the mogul field. Look for a *linked pathway* of three or four turns.
2. Start off slowly and swivel on the first mogul *summit*, then, as your speed increases, turn lower down the shoulder of the second and third moguls until you turn in the trough of the fourth. Ski out of that trough and *stop*.
3. Repeat this several times until you are confident that you can recognise the troughs, the hollow pathways, and that you can stop in control.
4. Your *perception* of the mogul field is now useful and your *emotions* will be appropriate for you to tackle a longer run. Set your target now at six turns, and try to get down into the hollow in the second turn.
5. Now link six turns with another six, but turn out of the first pathway and turn across the hill to keep your speed down, between each set of five or six turns.

   All your attention must, initially, be on your pathway. Have faith that your 'technique', your turning ability, can cope.

After several successful descents, you can sharpen up your technique by attending to *pressing against* and steering your *outer ski* of each and every turn.

Actively *press* against each instep successively as your eyes search out the hollow pathway at least two turns ahead of you.

Sarah Lewis works her legs quickly and independently to seek out the troughs, the linked hollows down a steep mogul field

Richard Siney, British artificial ski-slope champion, races giant slalom in Bulgaria

Konrad Bartelski leads Neal Nightingale at the last gate in a dual slalom at the All-England Championships

Racing

Skilful skiing implies versatile technical ability which can be applied with efficiency and effectiveness to demanding environmental situations.

Ski racing demands, and tests, skilful skiing.

The expanding racing programmes which are now developing from club level and from national level, on artificial ski slopes and local or Scottish snow, reflect the wishes of keen skiers of all ages to improve their skill and have it tested.

Racing on artificial ski slopes will extend you just when you think you have mastered the challenge of a uniform, homogeneous surface which requires more precision in your movements than snow does, but is often quite boring when you cannot find any challenges to meet. I hope I have set you many challenges in this book, but racing, on snow or artificial slopes, will set you more.

There are two forms of alpine racing which are accessible to British skiers: slalom and giant slalom.

Giant slalom

This is the easiest form of racing to begin but probably more difficult than others to do really well in.

The race course may be up to three-quarters of a mile long and consists of sweeping, round turns through forty to sixty gates with double poles. Racers will travel at between 30 and 50 mph on different parts of different courses.

Many aspects of giant slalom and slalom are very similar; the

110

differences lie in the higher speeds, longer courses and smoother turns of giant slalom. Great precision is required in aiming the skis, steering them and balancing. If mogul skiing is a major test of reaction and versatility in free skiing, giant slalom is a major test of courage, endurance and precision in 'free skiing'.

Established racers use different skis for giant slalom and slalom. This is not necessary for most keen skiers, however, because modern skis are made on a giant slalom 'model'. Changing skis is not very desirable either, from the point of view of familiarity. A new ski is another 'variable' to adapt to.

Slalom racing

This form of racing is available at most ski slopes and centres and you can train for it more easily than for giant slalom as it requires less space, lower speeds and fewer slalom poles.

Slalom courses in the Olympic games may have up to seventy-five gates for men and up to sixty for women, whereas 'fun' slaloms at your local slope may only have ten gates.

A minimum of fifteen gates is needed to get a true feel of slalom racing and over twenty gates are needed to put slalom racing ability to a true test.

Slalom course The course consists of pairs of poles and flags of the same colour. These pairs are called gates. They are placed

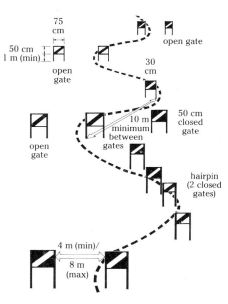

The giant slalom course, as laid down in FIS rule 900. The number of gates on the course is in proportion to the vertical drop

Slalom racing on an artificial ski-slope: a young Hayden Scott shows how

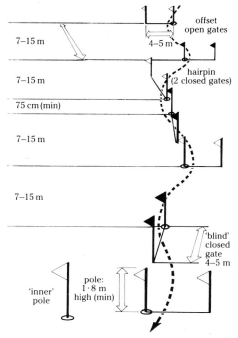

offset open gates

7–15 m

4–5 m

7–15 m

hairpin (2 closed gates)

75 cm (min)

7–15 m

7–15 m

'blind' closed gate 4–5 m

'inner' pole

pole: 1·8 m high (min)

The slalom course, as laid down in FIS rule 800

Dennis Edwards creates his own personal slalom course among a forest of poles. Initially confusing to the non-racer, this game quickly enables the skier to feel at home, comfortable and happy to be among slalom poles. This is an important pre-requisite to being a successful ski racer

alternately: *red* gate, *blue* gate, *red* gate, etc. The layout or design of the course is created uniquely for every race by the course setter, within the rules and guidelines of the F.I.S. (International Ski Federation).

Gates are placed in relation to the terrain, with great precision and with respect to the ability of the competitors so that they may combine maximum speed with control. The course will contain flowing, rhythmical pathways with varied combinations of gate patterns to test a wide variety of ski techniques, precision pathfinding and judgement, without the need for any sudden or sharp braking.

Some of the patterns of gates used in slalom races are shown in the diagrams, but in training you may make your own pathways, for slalom poles are coaches without words, providing only suggestions.

Playing with poles With your coach or simply just a few friends, you can set up some slalom poles which you can use to stimulate your skiing in many ways.

Slalom poles can be seen as obstacles to be avoided or, preferably, as indicators of pathways. Always look for the pathways around and between them.

Initially, slalom poles can be inhibiting. Even though each one only occupies about five square inches of the surface of the hillside they seem to cover the whole slope.

1. Set up a 'forest' of slalom poles, at random. Simply ski among them a few times and become familiar with them being there.
2. Look for pathways between the poles, and link your turns together, with a constant rhythm, aiming for the spaces between the poles. (See Chapter Six.)

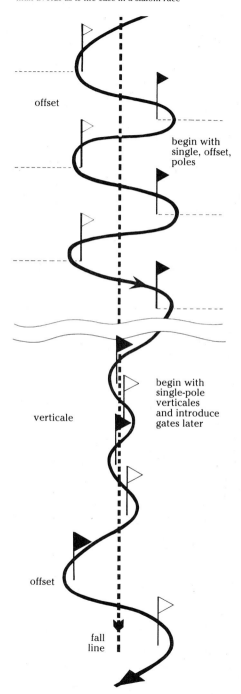

The conical corridor enables Dennis to improve his aiming along curved pathways, which are indicated ahead of him by the poles which he follows, rather than avoids as is the case in a slalom race

offset

begin with single, offset, poles

verticale

begin with single-pole verticales and introduce gates later

offset

fall line

3. Set a series in a straight line, each pole about five yards from the next one. Ski through every second space between the poles. Try to establish a good rhythm.

4. Repeat above, but with your feet apart.
Concentrate on pressing on one ski (instep) and then the other. Change the pressure quickly and cleanly.

These exercises will improve your aim and your agility, as well as helping you to become more aware of one of the 'fundamentals'—*pressure control*.

5. ***The conical corridor*** Plant the poles along an 'S' shape and incline them inwards like the sides of a cone. This will enable the legs to 'lean in' with appropriate angulation.

Leave a gap at the end of one turn and plant the next part of the 'S' on the inside of the next turn.

You always ski *outside* the poles.

This will help you become familiar with poles which cause you to aim along an arc and give you instant feedback, without 'crowding' you.

There seem to be a lot of poles *before* you set off but once you are skiing you realise they are not menacing—quite the contrary—in fact, they are comforting and supportive.

Further use of the poles

Develop the use of slalom poles so that you are always happy with them. They must not inhibit your skiing if you are to become very skilful.

1. Begin on easy terrain—well pisted.

2. When you begin to turn *around* the poles, use single poles or *open gates*, with an even rhythm.

3. On artificial slopes, set the gates offset from the fall-line and keep your turns round.

4. Introduce single poles and then, later, gated verticales. The turning poles should be approximately five to six metres apart.
5. Train with ten to twenty gate verticales.
6. Then add a couple of easy offset open gates at the end.
7. Practise attacking from offset gates into verticales (change of rhythm).
8. Practise attacking from verticales into offset gates.
9. Ski a gated, full course on *easy* terrain (initially twenty gates)—concentrate on accurate movements. Ski a good line.
10. Build a start platform and practise with a start wand.
11. Practise *sprinting* out of the start and through half a dozen gates, leave a space to *recover* and then *sprint again* through another six or so gates, and so on.
12. Use parallel slaloms for raising your attacking spirit and having fun.
13. Time your runs through *full courses*.

The training of children

As a member of the F.I.S. Youth and Children's Committee, I have been discussing the principles of training young racers with my colleagues.

There is increasing evidence that in many places *preparation training* is being wrongly introduced before *foundation training* has had its best effects. In particular, it has been noticed that *too much* 'pole' training inhibits the development of young racers.

To be complete and skilful racers, young children must become all-round skiers. Learning to cope with moguls and having *fun* in them, skiing off-piste and in variable snows will not only develop versatile techniques but improve courage, commitment and the ability to find pathways. You should do the same.

A more serious consequence of too much 'pole' training is the possibility of damage to young knees. Research into this is being conducted at present, but the evidence suggests that the use of longer skis, stiffer ski boots and bindings set too firmly (set for preventing broken bones but not injured ligaments or tendons) in hard, rutted slalom courses is causing too much stress on the knees, which formerly, with softer boots especially, was borne by the ankles and hips as well.

Young children should, therefore, train in courses which are changed often and in which the ruts are smooth and round. They should also use shortish skis, soft ski boots and be encouraged to think of their 'form', control and rhythm rather than their times.

Slalom training

There are three aspects to slalom racing which you can work on:

One: emotional disposition
Approach each race with a set routine
1. Inspect the course.

Below and *opposite page:*
Preparing herself mentally and physically for a race, Fiona Pulsford goes through her stretching routine, after a warm-up. Note that she wears her goggles well before the race, so that her eyes are completely adjusted to them before the start

2. Check all your equipment thoroughly.
3. Warm up and do some stretching exercises.
4. Assess your arousal level and 'psych' up or down accordingly (see Chapter Seven).
5. Remember your strong points and your successes in training—go to the start with a positive attitude.

Two: perception/tactics

Every race will be different, so you must study each course carefully in the inspection and decide how you will ski it. Look for the *changes in rhythm* and how you will recognise them in your approach, e.g. a specific gate combination, or terrain features.

Look for terrain features which you
1. might have problems with (drop aways on turns, for example)
2. can use to accelerate at (concave terrain and flowing gates).

When you approach the start gate and are preparing to go, concentrate on where—*precisely*—you are going to ski in the first 3–2–1 gates, then *go!*

On your way down, remain calm, don't think at all, *just watch the course ahead* and remember the 'guided missile' theory (Chapter Five). *Watch* for the parts of the course you noticed during inspection, and when they arrive, you *will* handle them.

If you do make a mistake, and everyone does in every race, it is how *you* cope with it that will determine your result.

Remember this: *mistakes are in the past.* You can do nothing about the mistake, so, above all, attend *now* to what is ahead of you and don't relax your concentration on the course ahead until after you have finished and stopped!

Once you have set off down the course, remember you are a 'guided missile'—you are guided not by your hopes and intentions but by the course ahead and the finish area. Keep your eyes *fixed* on your pathway, look at the terrain along which you are going to ski—'keep your eye on the ball', that is, on your pathway ahead! Small 'corrections' will be needed en route, but if you are 'intercepted' don't blame the missile, evaluate *why* you were intercepted and, in further training, modify the 'design and construction' of you, the missile.

Three: techniques

There are three parts of the course which you can train for—the *start*, the *turns*, and the *finish*.

A fast start The clock starts *when you open* the wand. Don't stand too close to it and open it before you are ready.

The fastest way to start is to use the 'kick start' developed by Jean-Claude Killy, which you can practise effectively on an artificial slope.

Place your ski sticks *firmly* in the slope below the wand. Feet apart and skis parallel, crouch down slightly, ready to spring.

When the starter says *'go'*, extend rapidly upwards and forwards, pressing hard down on your ski sticks which must be pointing slightly backwards. (This is where those push-ups come in useful!) Keep your body straight and aim to open the wand with the 'ankle angle' of your ski boot. You will be already well on your way when the clock starts.

Keep pushing on your ski sticks for as long as you can and pull your feet forward under you as you land (good job you've been doing the sit-ups!). Now bend at your hips and keep your arms close to your body for maximum thrust.

Skate if there is time, accurately, towards the first gate and turn early to put you on a good line. While you skate, pull your arms forward quickly to push again if there is time, or to 'hold your hoop' if there isn't.

The pace you set into the first gate will determine the tempo of your run.

Now that you are in the course the next consideration is 'the turns'.

You should attend, in training, both to your turning techniques and your timing and line.

The turns You will use many turning and gliding techniques and you will need a good coach or race trainer to help you master them all. We can look at two or three here.

Roddy Langmuir, 'Alpine Skier of the Year' in 1981, and member of the British Olympic team in 1980, did a significant part of his preparation training at Hillend in Edinburgh.
Your starting technique can be perfected also at your local 'permanent' skiing facility

116

To turn quickly yet smoothly, you must be agile, maintain independent leg action, and balance your *leg turning, edge change* and *pressure control* for every turn.

To steer your skis as accurately as possible *press* against the new outer ski and change its *edge*, as soon as possible. Keep good dynamic balance as you let your ski take you along a smooth arc. With practice, you will be able to carve a large proportion of your turns, turning your leg smothly to steer the ski on a smooth arc.

  ○ Edge your ski too little and you will sideslip—this is quite fast providing you don't slip low in the gate.
  ○ Turn your ski (leg) too much and you will skid—this is quite slow, whether you drop low or not.
  ○ Concentrate on the four fundamentals—PET and EPT with good dynamic balance.

Skating step 'turn' This sort of movement allows you to move quickly and positively from one foot to the other. It can be used to accelerate you on shallow terrain and it can enable you to gain height and step on to a higher line.

Don't use it for this unless you have to, though—remember you are trying to go *down* the hill quickly, so only step *up* the hill if you have slipped or skidded off your good line in the previous turn.

If your outer ski is carving at the end of the turn you will be able to start the next one easily.

Make sure your thigh is 'in' underneath you and you have a good edge hold. From a relatively low shape, *push* up and forwards off your carving ski and glide along your upper ski, now to become your new outer ski; as you increase *pressure* on it roll it over on to its inside *edge* and then *turn* it smoothly.

Foot forward It is normal to ski all the time with the ankles flexed forwards, but many of the world's best racers are using ankle flex 'in reverse', as it were, to help them achieve a smoother start to their turns.

The author demonstrates a skating step turn

Most top racers use summer training to practise or develop and refine the technical aspects of their skiing. Stig Strand, in summer training in Italy, practises sliding his foot forward to initiate the next turn smoothly. Note how his upper body is held forward as his feet move forward too

Dennis Edwards uses 'foot forward' sliding, to slice his new outer ski into the snow to begin the next turn. This movement aids good dynamic balance through the anticipation of a potential loss of balance, but it must be performed with good posture—pelvic tilt and 'hoop'

At the end of one turn, as you prepare to press against the new outer ski, slide that ski forwards, slightly ahead of you (do not sit back!) as you gently probe the snow, and then as you roll your ski over to change its edge, you will feel it *slice* into the snow. Your ankle will bend forwards again as the centrifugal effect of your momentum increases the pressure on the ski.

This small movement enables you to change edges very sensitively and will enable you to begin to carve early on an icy or very hard slope. It is useful also in ruts and in moguls.

Ruts When the course becomes rutted, you must ski with the rut. Even if the rut is a long way from the pole, stay in the rut. Take a short cut and you will end up hitting the wall of the rut square on, with disastrous consequences.

Approach the ruts with calm commitment, aim to find their rhythm and ski them like the trough in a mogul field.

Slide your outer ski forwards and into the *middle* of the rut. Press against your *instep* and steer the ski *with* the rut. *Too much* ankle bend may cause your bindings to release as the pressure from the rut builds up.

When you reach the middle, you can use the bank of the rut for

Nic Fellows recovers from a loss of balance in a soft snow rut and quickly attacks the next rut with confidence and accuracy. He had the second fastest time on this run of a race in Italy

Nicholas Redpath, junior international slalom racer, in Pamporova, Bulgaria, experiencing the 'conker effect'

support. This will give you a superb carving effect and you must anticipate the next phase of the turn, to keep good balance.

The rut will *squirt* your skis out and you must be ready to aim them into the middle of the next rut.

With practice and confidence you will be able to absorb the 'bumps' between ruts and keep your skis on the snow.

To ski ruts you must attack them with calmness and commitment.

The 'conker effect' Many racers are often told to 'get off their edges earlier'. By this, the trainer or coach usually means 'stop skidding or turning and begin the next turn'. We will look at 'line' in a moment but if you find yourself skidding a lot at the end of turns and you are not over-turning your legs, then you could be failing to use the 'conker effect'.

The 'conker effect' was discussed in Chapter Eleven. It is important in racing because at the point when you could be finishing your turn and 'getting off your edges' you will *feel and perceive* that you are resisting a sideways force.

What you can feel in your leg and foot is, indeed, a sideways force; it is the *centripetal* force which is impelling your turn. However, in this case feelings can be deceptive, because although

The commitment necessary to ski ruts successfully is clearly seen in Nic Fellows as he trains to cope with ruts in slalom courses

119

The 'conker' effect: a bird's eye view

you feel that if you relaxed you would fly *out* along the radius of your turn, in fact you would fly off at a *tangent* to it.

John loses control momentarily as he 'shrugs' his shoulders and closes his eyes as he passes the slalom pole. Note the weight thus moved on to his inner ski

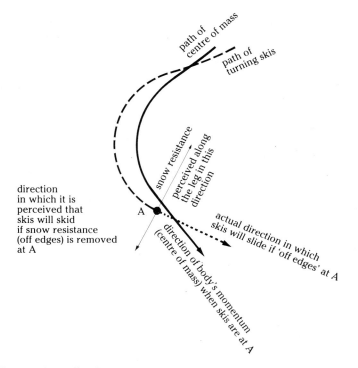

path of centre of mass

path of turning skis

snow resistance
perceived along
the leg in this
direction

direction
in which it is
perceived that
skis will skid
if snow resistance
(off edges) is removed
at A

A

actual direction in which
skis will slide if 'off edges' at A

direction of body's momentum
(centre of mass) when skis are at A

Fiona Pulsford, an excellent and attacking racer, here raises her arms too high, a defensive reflex, and so suffers slight loss of balance and loss of pressure on her outer, steering ski. Nevertheless, with eyes open and horizontal, and good posture, she went on to win the Girls' overall trophy in the 1980 Thomson Trophy Series

The 'conker effect', then, tells you that you need not hang on to your edges until you 'feel' the turn is finished. As soon as your skis are pointing into the new turn, get off your edges, relax your legs and let the 'conker effect' take your skis at a tangent to your last turn, on into your next one.

Passing the slalom poles One of the secrets of good racing is to pass close to the slalom poles but without hunching your shoulders or shying away from the pole as you pass it.

Brush the pole lightly and keep your eyes open, using your arm only to shield you from the pole.

If you keep your body shape firm, the pole will move as you pass by it.

Shrugging your shoulders will often cause you to lean onto your inside ski.

Don't let the pole disturb your balance as you pass it.

Some slalom poles are very flexible and it is possible to ski very close to them if you expect them to give. But will they? Every time you hit a slalom pole, momentum is lost (shared with the pole) and you may lose precious fractions of a second. If you are close to the pole, just ease it out of the way with *one arm*.

The F.I.S. has introduced new flexible, slalom poles in 1982 and I expect that more top racers will now hit the poles more often, but they will still maintain good balance and posture as they do so.

Timing and line *When you start* to turn and *where you aim*.

There are many variations on these points, depending upon your circumstances, but two general hints will help you improve your timing and line.

Malcolm Erskine, with excellent perception, technique and emotional disposition, takes a very tight line, which means that he will hit the slalom pole with his arm and his lower legs. The flexibility of these poles means that it will move easily out of his path. As more racers take such a line, high-standard gatekeepers are needed to differentiate between correct passages and incorrect passages when the feet go either side of the slalom pole

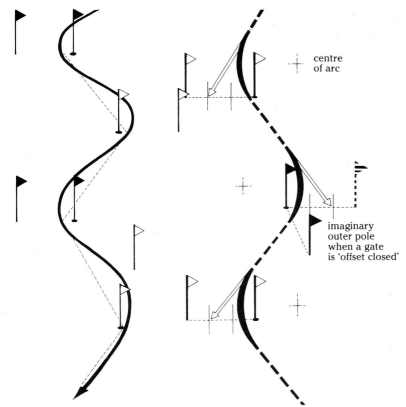

centre of arc

imaginary outer pole when a gate is 'offset closed'

Left: The curved solid line is the fastest line. Note how most of the turn is completed before passing the pole. The pole is *not* at the centre of the turn.
Right: Offset gates—aiming out of one turn at the *outer* third of the next gate

Where Logic would seem to indicate that the fastest line is the straightest. This is not so. The sudden changes of direction would slow you down. The fastest line will use round turns, the arcs having as large a radius as possible, without any sharp 'bends' in them.

In the diagram, the solid line shows the smoothest, fastest line.

That is the shape of the line, but where should it be in relation to the gates?

In general terms, you should aim off the inside pole when you start your turning arc. For offset gates, your 'conker effect' line, the tangent to your arc, should aim towards the outer third of an

Nigel Smith, in this gate at the British Junior Championships in 1980, displays excellent technique but poor judgement of line. The aimed path of his skis (A) would have caused his body to hit the gate, and thus he had to allow his skis to skid in the direction of arrow B in order to clear the gate without upsetting his balance too much. Many young racers, inexperienced in aiming their skis, lose precious seconds in this way

When skiing through closed gates close to the fall line, the 'exit line' from one gate aims at the *inner* third of the next (imaginary) gate

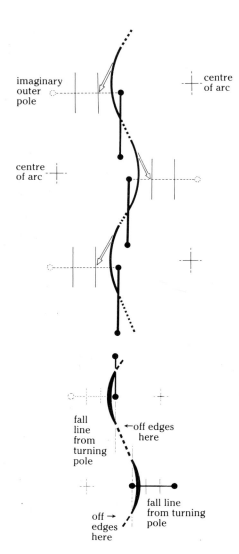

imaginary outer pole

centre of arc

centre of arc

fall line from turning pole

←off edges here

off → edges here

fall line from turning pole

open gate. (If it is not an open gate, imagine it is one to get the best aim.)

For gates closer to the fall line, aim for the inner third of the 'open' gate.

When The timing of your turns is easier than the aiming of your line.

You should be on your edge(s) and turning by the time you are directly above the turning pole and you should be off your edge and aiming for the next turn when your feet are directly below the slalom pole.

The finish Take the shortest line from the last gate to the finish and make one or two powerful skating steps. Bring your feet close together between skates, otherwise you may lose balance and fall between your skis.

A few powerful accurate skates are faster than many short ineffective ones.

Keep concentrating right across the finish line until you have stopped. *Only then* can you relax and look or listen for your time.

Competitive skiing will improve your technical turning ability, teach you why you should look after your equipment and how to use it properly and teach you how to handle ruts, moguls and variable snow conditions. Competition focuses your attention and concentration, helps you to learn more about yourself and improves your pathfinding ability. It will improve your confidence, give greater meaning to your practising and, most of all, it will give you a lot of fun.

Chapter thirteen

Cross-Country Skiing

Skiing as a recreation first became popular when Fridtjof Nansen, the Norwegian explorer, published his account in 1890 of crossing Greenland on skis. This was cross-country skiing, or Langlauf as it is sometimes known. Alpine skiing evolved from Langlauf, on the steeper terrain of the Alps, and grew to become the largest participant sport in Europe.

Using relatively cheap equipment, cross-country skiing is now gaining in popularity again. Quite apart from its value as a sport in its own right, cross-country skiing can have a part to play in the development of skilful alpine skiing.

I said in Chapter Six that the 'world' of the skier (alpine), being tilted, very slippy and relatively featureless, is different from the normal 'world' of the non-skier, which is flat, sticky and marked with straight lines. The world of the cross-country skier lies midway between these two, being flat but very slippy and sometimes marked with routes or pathways.

Cross-country skiing is an ideal introduction to the sport of alpine skiing for this reason and also because the equipment

'Making tracks' on a tilted, very slippy and relatively featureless world

Cross-country skiing gives a freedom of movement which enables you to explore the mountains and develop your snowcraft

allows more 'normal' movements to be made, with lighter and more comfortable boots and skis.

Cross-country skiing has as its keystone the ability to run on skis, using both legs independently and balancing in movement on a narrow and slippy base. X-C skiing, as it is known, provides the ideal foundation training of dynamic balance on slippy feet, using familiar human movements, adapted to the equipment.

The growth in popularity of X-C skiing means that you can now hire the equipment and have lessons when you go on holiday, but the logistics of equipment organisation mean that it is unlikely that you will find many places willing and happy to hire you both X-C and alpine equipment consecutively during your holiday. An exception to this is in the Federal Republic of Germany where, following the work of Gattermann, Kuchler and Mair, ski schools actively encourage combined courses of two days' X-C and three days' alpine skiing.

It is my belief that if you hire a pair of X-C skis for a few days when you next visit the Alps or, better still, purchase a pair and use them locally when the snow falls, you will soon develop an independence of leg turning and sensitivity of pressure control, edge change and dynamic balance which will enhance your alpine skiing. Skiing down gentle pistes on X-C skis will also raise your emotional disposition and provide an excitement possible on alpine skis only at higher speeds.

Parallel skiing

For many years now, ski schools have brainwashed the public into believing that parallel turns were the ultimate goal in skiing. Parallel turns on X-C skis are easy to do, if you use a modified 'compression' turning technique, which keeps your heels firmly on the skis. More importantly, however, X-C skiing requires step turns, step turns which rely on delicate balance and good control of the other three 'fundamentals' and step turns which form the basis of good technique for competitive alpine skiers.

At the 1979 Inter-ski Congress in Zao, Japan, Erhard Gattermann told of a researcher whose work it was to examine all the film and television coverage of world championship (alpine) racing in order to select 'ideal form' parallel turns for the current ski teaching manual. Unfortunately, they had to change their whole illustration plan, because this researcher could not find one single clear illustration of the pure parallel turn among the many thousands of turns made at the world championships by the world's top racers.

Racers and good skiers alike change pressure accurately and decisively with more or less of a stepping action, from one foot to another.

X-C skiing introduces, on a slippy world, the basic movements of the world's best skiers and so provides a good foundation training as well as giving a lot of pleasure in its own right.

The competitive cross-country racer is more like the middle-distance runner than the downhill racer

Competitive cross-country skiing

Many more medals are awarded at the Olympic Games for X-C skiing in its various forms than for alpine skiing.

There are six categories of alpine racing, although it is hoped that freestyle will soon be introduced as an Olympic event.

There are ten categories involving X-C skiing, excluding the jumping events which, together with the X-C events, are known collectively as *Nordic skiing*.

The typical build of the successful X-C competitor is like that of a middle/long distance runner and your aerobic capacity and lactic acid tolerance are more likely to determine your ultimate potential as an X-C competitor than your ski technique. At the competitive levels, X-C skiing diverges greatly from alpine skiing and, for this reason, you are advised to seek specialist advice from the English Ski Council or the Scottish National Ski Council if you wish to pursue X-C skiing at a competitive level.

The basic techniques are easily mastered by all and may be practised at home on roller skis if local snow is not available, and X-C skiing will complement your alpine skiing in a very positive

Good balance and basic techniques, as well as a lot of fun, can be learned on roller skis and asphalt pathways in summer in your own locality

Alex Leaf enjoys the exhilaration of skilful off-piste skiing

way. It will improve the width of your perceptions, enhance your emotional disposition and increase the sensitivity of your technique. It will enhance your skilful skiing.

One final thought
Skiing is, ultimately, all about having fun, taking pleasure from skilful movements and being in a beautiful though sometimes hostile environment. But man is a social animal and skiing should never be done alone. Always ski with friends and enjoy each other's company and shared experiences in the mountains.

Skilful skiing will enable you to ski with more people in more and varied places. Skilful skiing will enrich your experiences and give greater value and meaning to your recreation.

I wish you skilful skiing always! Have fun.